RUSI DEFENCE STUDIES SERIES

General Editor David Bolton, Director, Royal United Services Institute for Defence Studies

Editor Dr Brian Holden Reid

Questions on defence give rise to emotion, sometimes to the detriment of balanced judgement. Since 1831 the Royal United Services Institute for Defence Studies has been noted for its objectivity, independence and initiative; the views of its members sharpened by responsibility and experience. In continuance of the Institute's aims, the *RUSI Defence Studies Series* seeks to provide a wider understanding and better informed debate of defence and national security issues. However, the views expressed in the books are those of the authors alone.

Published

Richard Clutterbuck
THE FUTURE OF POLITICAL VIOLENCE:
Destabilization, Disorder and Terrorism

Christopher Coker
NATO, THE WARSAW PACT AND AFRICA
THE FUTURE OF THE ATLANTIC ALLIANCE
US MILITARY POWER IN THE 1980s

Michael Hobkirk
THE POLITICS OF DEFENCE BUDGETING: A Study of Organisation and Resource Allocation in the UK and USA

Clive Rose
CAMPAIGNS AGAINST WESTERN DEFENCE:
NATO's Adversaries and Critics

Forthcoming

Michael Leifer (editor)
THE BALANCE OF POWER IN EAST ASIA

David Greenwood
BRITAIN'S DEFENCE PRIORITIES

E. S. Williams
THE SOVIET MILITARY: Political Education, Training and Morale

James Sherr
SOVIET POWER AND PROSPECTS

THE FUTURE OF POLITICAL VIOLENCE
Destabilization, Disorder and Terrorism

Richard Clutterbuck

First published 1986

Published by
THE MACMILLAN PRESS LTD
Houndmills, Basingstoke, Hampshire RG21 2XS
and London
Companies and representatives
throughout the world

Typeset by
Wessex Typesetters
Frome, Somerset

**Printed in Great Britain
at the University Printing House, Oxford**

British Library Cataloguing in Publication Data
The Future of political violence: destabilization,
disorder and terrorism
1. Violence
I. Clutterbuck, Richard
322.4′2   JC328.6
ISBN 0–333–37989–6
ISBN 0–333–37990–X Pbk

Contents

Preface

During 1983, the Royal United Services Institute and Control Risks Information Services brought together an unusual mixture of four kinds of people at two one-day conferences to discuss the future of political violence. The RUSI attracted its normal membership from the armed forces, the police and the civil service while CRIS brought in a distinguished body of about 100 senior executives from the business world. The resulting discussions (some in plenary sessions and some in seminar) produced a range of ideas far wider than would be normal at a less broadly based conference.

Both conferences were chaired by the Director of the RUSI, Group Captain David Bolton. The platform speakers included Sir Robert Mark, formerly Commissioner of the Metropolitan Police; Mr John Dellow, Assistant Commissioner, Crime, at Scotland Yard, who commanded the Iranian Embassy siege in London in 1980; Brigadier (now Major-General) Peter de la Billiere, who has served in various posts in the Special Air Service up to 1983; Dr Hans Josef Horchem, who was a Director of the *Verfassungsschutz* (the German equivalent of the Security Service or MI5); and Professor Paul Wilkinson, Professor of International Relations at Aberdeen University and a leading writer on terrorism. Transcripts of their talks form Part III of this book.

Also, at each of the two conferences, the research staff from CRIS gave up-to-date surveys of the political stability and security risks around the world. At the second conference this was done in separate seminars to allow more time for discussion by those most interested in the particular parts of the world. For this book. CRIS have written updated surveys and forecasts and these comprise Part II.

I have not presumed to edit Part III at all. The transcripts are as submitted or recorded and approved by the speakers and, despite some overlap with the review or with each other, I believe that the reader will prefer to have each as a complete and independent contribution from a leading authority in his own field.

These contributions were short (each about 20 minutes) so the majority of the time on both days was spent in discussion. As rapporteur I decided that, rather than attempt to record and summarize these discussions in detail, I should write a review of the whole subject and this forms Part I of the book. I also spoke from the platform myself at both meetings, and I have incorporated what I said in Part I rather than in a separate transcript in Part III. I have not attributed anything in Part I either to the speakers or to participants from the floor and it is, in fact, my interpretation of what I learned from these two days of stimulating and wide-ranging discussions. No one else can therefore be blamed for the views expressed in it, and I hope that it makes a more coherent whole than if I had written it as 'minutes of the meeting'.

The review is intended to be a working paper for use by people concerned with the realities of planning the protection of themselves, their families, their homes, their products and their premises, governmental, industrial or commercial, against the likely patterns of violent crime and of political violence by demonstrators, rioters and terrorists, both in industrial and Third World countries, in the years ahead. Different people (for example, government, industrial or commercial executives, security staffs or intelligence or police officers) will be concerned with different aspects, so I have tried to make the chapters stand on their own as far as possible, where necessary repeating some of the essentials (for example, the nature of Shia terrorism or of the new 'diffuse' guerrilla philosophy in Europe or the problems of reconciling protection and security with civil liberties) with a fairly full table of contents, rather than burden the reader with too many cross-references.

July 1985   RICHARD CLUTTERBUCK
                                          Exeter and London

Notes on the Contributors

PART I

RICHARD CLUTTERBUCK retired from the Army as a Major General in 1972 and taught international politics and political violence at the University of Exeter from 1972 to 1983. He lectures regularly to police and business audiences and has given over 200 broadcasts. He has written 11 other books.

PART II

PETER JANKE is Head of Research at Control Risks Ltd, London, where he analyses political risk. He lectures at military and police establishments and is the author of *Guerrilla and Terrorist Organisations: a World Directory and Bibliography*.

ALISON CONNORTON is Middle East and North African research analyst at Control Risks Ltd, London. She formerly worked at the Japanese Nomura Research Institute.

DAVID FANTHORPE analyses political risk in Africa South of the Sahara for Control Risks Ltd, London. His previous career was in the Department of Education and Science.

JAMES ANDERSON is Latin American research analyst at Control Risks Ltd, London. He formerly worked at the Institute for the Study of Conflict. Publications include *The Caribbean Strategic Vacuum*.

JOHN BRAY is Asian Research Analyst and Librarian at Control Risks Ltd, London. He has taught in Africa and India and contributes to journals on Asian affairs.

Part III

HANS JOSEF HORCHEM served as a Judge in the Rhineland in 1955–57 and then worked with the Federal Office for the Protection of the Constitution (the *Verfassungschutz*), first in Cologne and then as Director in Hamburg.

SIR ROBERT MARK joined the Manchester City Police in 1937, was appointed Chief Constable of Leicester in 1957 and Commissioner of the Metropolitan Police in London in 1972, retiring in 1977.

JOHN DELLOW joined the City of London Police in 1951. He was in command of the siege of the Iranian Embassy at Princes Gate in London in 1980 and is currently Assistant Commissioner (Crime) at Scotland Yard.

PAUL WILKINSON was Senior Lecture in Politics at University College, Cardiff, and is now Professor of International Relations at the University of Aberdeen. He writes and broadcasts regularly on terrorism.

PETER DE LA BILLIERE is a Major-General in the British Army. He held various posts in the Special Air Service (SAS) until December 1982 and is now Military Commissioner and Commander British Forces in the Falkland Islands.

Abbreviations

Note: For foreign acronyms and in other cases where it is judged to be more helpful to the reader, an English description (in parentheses) is given instead of spelling out the words.

AD Direct Action (left-wing terrorist movement in France)

ANC African National Congress (South Africa)

ASALA (International Armenian terrorist group, anti-Turkish)

BBE (Anti-terrorist force in the Netherlands)

BEFA (Computerized intelligence system in West Germany)

BfV (Federal political intelligence service in West Germany)

BKA (Federal police intelligence service in West Germany)

BND (Foreign intelligence service in West Germany)

BR Red Brigades (left-wing terrorist group in Italy)

CCC Combatant Communist Cells (in Belgium)

CLODO (Anti-computer movement in France)

CMC Crisis Management Committee

COBRA (Government crisis management organization in UK)

CPM Communist Party of Malaya

CPT Communist Party of Thailand

CRIS Control Risks Information Services

DGI (Cuban intelligence service)

EEC European Economic Community

EPLF Eritrean Peoples Liberation Front

ETA (Violent Basque separatist movement in Spain)

FMLN (Left-wing terrorist amalgam in El Salvador)

FNLC (Corsican Liberation Front in France)

FRAP (Left-wing terrorist movement in Spain)

FRELIMO (Government political party in Mozambique)

GRAPO (Left-wing anti-terrorist movement in Spain)

GSG9 (Anti-terrorist force in West Germany)

IR Infra Red

IRA Irish Republican Army

JCAG Justice Commandos for the Armenian Genocide

KANU (Government political party in Kenya)

KDP Kurdish Democratic Party

LNT Local Negotiating Team

MNLF Moro National Liberation Front

MPAIAC (Canary Islands independence movement)

MPLA (Government political party in Angola)

NBC Nuclear, Biological and Chemical (warfare or weapons)

NORAID (Irish–American movement supporting the IRA)

NPA New People's Army (Philippines)

NRA National Resistance Army (Uganda)

OPEC Organization of Petroleum Exporting Countries

OPM (Papuan independence movement in Indonesia)

PAS (Militant Islamic Party in Malaysia)

PIRA Provisional Irish Republican Army

PL Front Line (left-wing terrorist movement in Italy)

PLO Palestine Liberation Organization

POLISARIO (West Saharan independence movement in Morocco)

PUK Patriotic Union of Kurdistan

PULO Pattani United Liberation Organization (Thailand)

RAF Red Army Faction (left-wing terrorist movement in West Germany)

RNM (Resistance movement in Mozambique)

RSS (Militant Hindu organization in India)

RZ Revolutionary Cells (left-wing terrorist movement in West Germany)

SADR (Political front of POLISARIO, q.v.)

SAS Special Air Service

SDLP Social Democratic and Labour Party (Northern Ireland)

SL Luminous Path (left-wing terrorist movement in Peru)

SPLA Sudan People's Liberation Army

SWAPO South West African People's Organization

TI Thermal Imagery

TL (Catalan independence movement in Spain)

TPLA Turkish People's Liberation Army

TREVI (EEC government's anti-terrorist organization)

UAE United Arab Emirates

UNITA (Anti-government guerrilla movement in Angola)

VSBD (Neo-Nazi group in West Germany)

ZANU Zimbabwe African National Union

Part I

Review: The Next Ten Years

1 The Spectrum of Dissent and Political Violence

DESTABILIZATION: THE NAME OF THE GAME

No one who has lived through a revolution, or even a temporary collapse of order in a city, will have any doubts about how slender is the bulwark between civilization and chaos. The past ten years have seen many horrifying examples, such as the disintegration of Lebanon, Nicaragua and El Salvador into prolonged civil war and the sudden crumble of the Shah's regime in Iran in 1978–79 leading to one of the most totalitarian and bloodthirsty tyrannies in the world.

Totalitarian regimes seem to be the most secure in the short term, largely because of their pervasive and non-accountable intelligence services and their monopoly of their own media, but, in the longer term, they are brittle. The Soviet Union is the longest contemporary totalitarian survivor and has not yet accomplished even the normal human life-span of three score years and ten.

Authoritarian societies, which differ from the totalitarian in that their peoples are required to keep out of politics rather than to practise a particular ideology, seem, perhaps surprisingly, to be more vulnerable. The Shah's Iran and Caetano's Portugal were authoritarian rather than totalitarian. The most resilient in the long run are the liberal democracies though, if their equilibrium is shattered their chaos can be prolonged, witness the agony of Lebanon.

Where there has been a collapse of order as in Lebanon, Iran, Nicaragua or El Salvador, the continuance of diplomatic and commercial activities has become hazardous and sometimes

3

impossible. Lesser degrees of disorder can produce similar diplomatic and commercial hazards. A crumbling of judicial or police morale and efficiency can quickly remove the fear of conviction amongst rioters, criminals and terrorists and thereby unleash a threat to which both individuals and installations become nakedly vulnerable. The surprising thing is that this kind of disorder does not occur more often, but no one should be complacent about how quickly an explosion of crime or mob violence can develop. The name of the game is destabilization.

Liberal democracies, even if the most resilient in the long term, are the most vulnerable to destabilization in the short term. Freedom of speech gives minorities the scope for bringing their views to the attention of others. Their failure to persuade the majority to accept these views is all the more galling and frustrating because the channels for persuasion, through elected assemblies, the media and the right to demonstrate collectively in public, do exist but the public obstinately declines to be persuaded. So the dissenters, frustrated and humiliated, turn to indirect, illegal or violent means: to misrepresentation, deception or betrayal of trust; or to rioting, burning, bombing, kidnapping or killing.

It is rare in a democracy for the dissenters actually to overthrow a government by these means; they therefore pin their hopes on destabilizing it: by undermining the morale of ministers, officials and police; by provoking them to over-react; and by driving the public to lose confidence in both the will and the ability of the government to control the situation and, fearing for the safety of their families, to clutch in desperation at the lifeline of a totalitarian or authoritarian leadership which seems to know what it wants to do and offers the best hope of restoring order. The dissenters, even if they do not share its power, know that the new regime will be more brittle and less resilient than the democracy it has replaced.

Most of the violence which threatens families, corporate staffs (expatriate and local) diplomats and officials, however, is not part of any calculated plot to overthrow the state. Most of it does come from the frustration of these dissenting minorities, from social deprivation and, above all, from crime. There are, sadly, indications that all of these are likely to increase.

SOCIAL VIOLENCE AND CRIME

In the cities of both the industrialized and developing world, there are growing numbers of young people who have not much to do, not much to spend and, not surprisingly, no feeling whatever of respect for the values of the society which has placed them in that situation. In the more affluent societies, feeling bitter and cheated, they turn to vandalism as an escape from boredom and then to petty crime as source of both excitement and money. In the shanty towns of the Third World, they often have no legal source of income at all, so crime becomes their only means of sustenance. In both cases, there is a wide choice of targets both for vandalism and crime so families and organizations which take manifestly better than average security precautions are unlikely to be selected. Such precautions will in any case be a necessary basis for protection against the violence of rioters and terrorists and against more serious crime.

Riots can arise from social, industrial and political causes and these will be discussed in later chapters and in some of the resource papers. Serious crime for material gain, stealing, kidnapping, maiming and killing, requires the same protection as the same kind of attacks from political terrorists, and this too, with the aims and motivation of the terrorists, will be discussed later.

THE ESCALATION OF POLITICAL VIOLENCE

The violence arising from frustration in the concrete jungles in affluent societies, or in the shacks on the fringes of the cities of the Third World, is mainly a small group phenomenon. Sometimes, however, it can be politically exploited, by either the left or the right, especially with an ethnic or religious appeal as in Spain or Northern Ireland. Most of the violence with a calculated political aim, however, is conducted or at least organized by people with the sophistication to make such political calculations. Since this sophistication is usually acquired only by children brought up in comfortable homes, their frustration as teenagers and as young men and women arises not so much from material deprivation as from a reaction against the values of their parents, their schools, and the society into which they see themselves being projected. Typically, this reaction develops most when they are students. At this stage they are often genuinely idealistic and concerned about the inequalities of modern society, and they join in protest movements. After a time they become disillusioned at finding that protest marches have little effect; many drop out of the movement but others make their demonstrations more disruptive and violent in the hope of at least attracting more attention to their cause. When this achieves nothing, more of them are discouraged and drop out but a hard core may escalate the violence to burning or bombing the 'symbols of capitalism'. This may result in casual and probably unintended killing, usually of the wrong people, like retired workers acting as watchmen. Again, many are disgusted and drop out but a hard core go on to selective kidnapping and murder of judges, bankers, industrialists and the like.

The aims and techniques of these various degrees of activity from protest to street violence and terrorism, and the motivation and development of those who do them, will be discussed in the appropriate chapters. So will the development and motivation of the rather different type of terrorist to be found in nationalist or ethnic movements such as ETA or the IRA.

In most European countries, a deep rooted desire for security and tranquillity amongst the overwhelming majority of people, and the efficiency of the police and intelligence services, eventually result in a decline of politically violent movements until they die out or their activity reaches a level comparable with that of normal violent crime. This has been the trend both amongst revolutionary terrorists in Germany and Italy and amongst ethnic or nationalist terrorists in Northern Ireland or Spain. Sometimes, as in Portugal in 1974–75, a Marxist movement has actually gained power out of violence and chaos and has then been ousted by concerted action by moderate democratic parties with popular support but this full circle has been rare.

In the Third World, and especially in Latin America, the pattern has generally been more violent and the political swings more extreme. The collapse of order degenerates into civil war in which either a left wing movement seizes and retains power (as in Nicaragua) or is ousted by a right wing, usually military, reaction. Occasionally, as in Argentina, these lurches have eventually led to a genuine restoration of elective democracy but this too has been rare.

The effects of coming technological developments on the nature of societies and on the techniques of protest, public disorder, crime and terrorism, are discussed in Chapters 2 to 5. The problems of international cooperation, the response to street violence and terrorism by governments, and the relationships between civil authorities, the judiciary, the police, the armed forces and the intelligence agencies, are discussed in Chapters 6 and 7 and in a number of the Resource Papers. The corporate response to the various threats is discussed in Chapter 8, with some guidelines for security, contingency planning and crisis management in the light of the anticipated changes in society and technology in the coming ten years.

2   Protest, Riots and Industrial Conflict

THE WORLD OF THE 1990s

The next ten years will see the maturing of the microelectronics boom. Since the early 19th century a series of 50-year cycles has been clearly discernible: 20–25 years of depression during which a new technology is developed have usually been followed by 20–25 years of boom as that technology works its way through industry and reaches its peak. The demands of a rising standard of living then gradually overtake the expansion of the economy which stagnates and relapses into another depression, during which necessity stimulates research and the seeds of a fresh technological revolution are sown. Examples were the railway boom of the 1850s and 1860s followed by the slump of the 1880s; the chemical electrical and mass production boom of the early 20th century followed by the slump of the 1930s; and the electronic, automation and mass air transport boom of the 1950s and 1960s followed by the depression of the 1970s and 1980s. This depression is stimulating the current galloping development of microelectronics which will work its way through productive and service industries to reach its peak in the 1990s.

Each of these transitions has brought its stresses and strains on society and each brought dramatic changes in work patterns and lifestyles. The microelectronics revolution will do the same.

By the mid 1990s, industrial working hours should be down to a 30-hour or four-shift week, producing more real wealth than is currently produced in a 40-hour week. Many more people will be in service industries and more of them will work at home through computer and cable television networks. Leisure industries will have grown dramatically and transport will be used more for pleasure and less for commuting or business trips, provided that the more efficient economy produces the surplus wealth to underwrite them.

Ordinary people will have access to a flood of instant information. This will give increased power over people's minds to those who control the mass-communications media. It will strengthen the power of governments, but also that of those who wish to undermine them except where governments deny them access to the myriad of communication channels which will reach into people's homes. The equation will vary from country to country; totalitarian governments will be able to tighten their control over their populations; liberal societies will experience a growing conflict between the power of their government and the increasingly articulate and bitter opposition of its critics, who will have access to the vastly expanded means of disseminating their views.

Inequalities will stretch, in both the old and the new industrial countries, between the 'haves' who learn to use the information explosion and the 'have-nots' who, having scorned or otherwise failed to take the opportunities to qualify for the more rewarding kinds of brain work, will seek solace in cheap entertainment and do dismal jobs or none at all; there will be a new 'them' and a new 'us'.

An immense amount of personal data will be recorded and stored. Civil rights pressure may give the individual increasing access to his own data but it will not stem the flood of information. If it were to prove possible to provide effective safeguards against their misuse, all of these capabilities would be potentially beneficial but, on balance, though they will increase affluence, they will probably also increase the alienation of dissenting minorities. Societies will generally become more divided, less liberal and more brittle.

Another product of affluence and dissent will be the continued growth of the drug culture. Societies will be able to afford more generous social security payments for the inevitably large numbers of unemployed. Embittered by boredom and by envy or rejection of the affluent of the society around them, and with fewer and fewer moral inhibitions about theft, they will go to any lengths to find money to escape from reality into soft and hard drugs. Drug-taking, and the desperate crime which underwrites it, may reach alarming proportions both amongst educated dissidents and amongst the 'no-hopers' who dropped out of the race at school.

The gap in per capita GNP between rich and poor countries will also increase. Third World populations will soar, especially in the cities; by the end of the century, it is likely to double or even treble in places like Calcutta and Mexico City, whose populations may reach 20 or 30 million. This population growth rate in many countries is already nullifying their economic growth rate. Feeding these enormous urban populations will present appalling problems, not so much in growing the food but in transporting it and in providing gainful employment for the mass of people in the shanty towns who need to buy it.

Energy will also present a problem of distribution in Third World countries. Overall, however, even if the consumption of oil reserves is causing concern before the end of the century, this very concern will have stimulated development of other forms of energy which will in turn become more economic as impending shortage pushes up the price of oil. There is not, therefore, likely to be any serious shortage of energy in the industrial countries.

The pattern of dissent, public disorder, crime and terrorism cannot but be influenced by these changes in the pattern of work and living in the coming ten years. In Third World countries, growing desperation and lawlessness amongst the sprawling urban populations and bitterly disappointed expectations amongst the new student generations will be highly destabilizing, and ripe for exploitation by those who wish to fuel this destabilization in order to cause governments friendly to the West to be overthrown, or to make conditions unviable for continued operation of multinational corporations.

The most threatening development in the Third World is the resurgence of Islamic fundamentalism, which is likely to gain rather than lose momentum because of its appeal to the poorer elements (especially those of the Shia sect) in Islamic societies whose religion teaches them to blame their plight on modern technology and Western materialism. Fundamentalist leaders, like other religious fanatics in the past, have little respect for the lives of their supporters or of their enemies, so this is likely to be a growing source of disruption of Western activities in the

Middle East, both of governments and of multinational corporations; also of increasingly ruthless terrorism, not only in the Middle East but also spreading into Europe. The only mitigating factor is that the regimes of its two main bases, Iran and Libya, are very unpopular in most of the Arab world except for Syria and South Yemen. The prognosis for Shia terrorism and for the stability of the Arab world are more fully examined in Part II.

The changes in the pattern of life and employment in industrial countries is likely to lead to increases in industrial conflict, in protest and possibly in violence against the sinews and symbols of the microelectronic era, notably the computer and communications networks. There will be two main and contrasting sources for this disruption and violence. Industrial conflict will be generated by an affluent workforce, with an increasing proportion of white-collar workers, exploiting their own ability to forego their pay without immediate hardship and their realization that the price of disruption of high technology industries by a small number of people is so high that managements will be tempted to buy them off. Political protest, on the other hand, will be generated more by people who have had the educational opportunities to participate in the more affluent modern society but prefer to reject its values for ideological and environmental reasons. This rejection may take the form of disruption, sabotage or malicious damage, perhaps escalating to bombing, personal attack and other forms of terrorism.

INDUSTRIAL CONFLICT

The industrial conflicts in Britain and Germany in mid-1984 gave convincing proof both of the ability of affluent workers to endure long strikes and of the economic vulnerability of modern society. The only real restraint was the fear of loss of employment which, once lost, might never be regained. As the microelectronic revolution brings its boom, with more people earning more money, working shorter hours, and so having time to spare, both the affluence and the opportunities for disruption will increase. Militant leaders will be tempted to strengthen their following by extracting large short term benefits for their members from employers who will be anxious to avoid the even greater cost of disruption of their operations, with consequent long term losses both to the industries and to those working in them. While new industrial relations laws may provide some restraint, the only real cure will be greater participation by the shop-floor in management decisions, not so much by trade union representatives, who fear that their bargaining position would be eroded by such participation, but by representatives directly elected by secret ballot on the shopfloor. Experience in Germany and Japan has proved that these elected representatives are best able to convince the workforce that killing (or weakening) their own industry will in the end be counterproductive to their own interests. Though good management communication can contribute a great deal, this realization must ultimately come within the workforce itself.

PROTEST AND VIOLENT DEMONSTRATIONS

There is a very wide range of sources of political protest and these will multiply rather than decline. Closely related to industrial conflict is protest by interest groups which see their prosperity and prospects being eroded (like French farmers and truck drivers in 1984). As the pace of change in society increases, so the numbers who see themselves affected in this way will grow, and they will more often resort to disruption. In the future, their targets may be telecommunications rather than blocking movement by road.

Also associated with industrial conflict will be protests arising from the belief that computer technology is the main cause of job losses. Unemployment in the next ten years is likely to remain high because of the traditional reluctance of trade unions to link higher earnings to higher productivity. This will inhibit the only real solution to the problem, for instance, work sharing in which more people work shorter hours and make full use of modern technology to produce more output (in the form of goods or services) in less time at competitive cost. Unless there is a major change of heart in the West European countries (notably in Britain) they are likely to be increasingly squeezed out by Japan and by the newly industrializing countries in East and South East Asia, such as Singapore, Malaysia, Taiwan,

Korea and Thailand – and possibly also China by the end of the century.

Conflict between communities – racial, tribal, nationalist, secessionist or religious – shows no sign of abating in the world. For the reasons given earlier, the inequalities in all societies will stretch rather than converge, and the tools for state control and repression will become more powerful, so these kinds of conflict may become more bitter.

Other groups of protesters which are likely to grow are those generated by pacifism and environmentalism (which link the opposition to nuclear weapons and to nuclear power). Closely related to these are those who will protest against what they will see as the constant erosion of privacy and civil liberties by the extension of recording and use of personal data. Computer networks will be their prime target.

Finally, all of these kinds of protest will be exploited by people who have the wider political aim of destabilizing Western democratic societies as a whole for ideological reasons. Their techniques, already well proven, may be to select a sympathetic issue, such as one of those described above, and exploit it to gather a wide base of support. Alternatively – and sometimes indistinguishably – they may jump on the bandwagon of a protest movement already well under way, and try to radicalize it from within. In either case, the tactics will be to bring about confrontations by creating situations in which the police have no choice other than to use force or to allow a collapse of order with unacceptable risks to life and property. The aim of the organizers is that this confrontation will get people aroused, polarized and committed to their cause. If thereafter they can develop a momentum leading to more widespread disorder, they may hope to over-stretch the police reinforcement system so that, to prevent things getting out of hand, harassed police officers in inadequate strength will use excessive force, thereby escalating the violence, the anger, the disorder and the destabilization. The most important target will be to erode and if possible to do irrevocable damage to the cooperative relationship between the police and the majority of the people.

RIOTS

Industrial disputes and political demonstrations can degenerate into riots but other riots may arise spontaneously from social causes, as occurred all over England in 1981. These spontaneous riots usually explode in deprived and declining areas of inner cities and the indications are that, in most West European countries and possibly also in the USA, the changing nature of society will make such explosive situations more likely. There are four main reasons to expect this. Firstly, the coloured immigrant population in Western Europe will increase, even if further immigration is curtailed, due to the expanding families of those already there. Secondly, this will raise the black/white ratio to a more explosive mixture, arousing more white fears and resentment in the poorer housing districts. Thirdly the inequalities between rich and poor (poor white as well as poor black) will widen, further increasing the resentment and the tension. Fourthly, a growing body of more educated dissidents, rejecting the society created by the microelectronics revolution, will (as they sometimes do now) fish in troubled waters by exacerbating the tensions, especially between young blacks and the police, in order to further the process of destabilization.

The evolution and chemistry of these explosive situations is now well established. As more affluent city workers move to the suburbs, an inner ring of old and crumbling houses, interspersed with low-cost blocks of flats, develops between the thriving city centre and the comfortable garden suburbs. In this inner ring, poorer tenants pay lower rents so councils and landlords have less to spend on repair and maintenance. As standards fall, anyone who can afford to move out does so, and still poorer people move in, more and more of them black. As more blacks move in more whites move out and the inner rings become ghettos of poor blacks mingled with a residue of unwilling and embittered poor whites. Unemployment rises, especially among those in their late teens. To escape from the poverty and boredom of their crowded family flats, they gang up in the streets, and turn to petty crime. The crime rate draws heavier policing, increasing the resentment ('why pick on us all the time?'). Hatred between the police and young blacks (sometimes joined by equally frustrated young whites) builds up – and it needs only a spark, usually arising from routine police patrolling against crime, to set off an explosion. The scale of such explosions shook Britain in the summer of 1981, in a series of riots in which there were 3000 arrests and more than 1500 policemen injured.

As the boom gathers momentum in the late 1980s and 1990s, this kind of explosion will become more rather than less likely, for the reasons given above and also because the more affluent society, with higher social security providing a higher poverty line, will create a climate in which bored and frustrated people may be more willing to risk taking to violence on the streets. It is axiomatic that rising affluence leads to rising violence and crime.

THE ROLE OF THE MEDIA IN CIVIL DISORDER

Television generally has a malignant rather than a restraining effect on public order and this is likely to increase in the future as channels proliferate and news spreads faster, and in more dramatic form, into people's homes. Television already reinforces prejudices and inflames conflicts rather than cooling them. In industrial disputes the contending parties take up public positions from which it is difficult to withdraw. Television provides the incentive for demonstrations and, once the cameras are there, their presence incites people to 'act up' to gain attention for their cause. The copycat syndrome was much in evidence in 1981 whereby bored young people were fired by television news pictures to go out and riot or loot. Multichannel television and instant news will increase each one of these phenomena in the years to come.

CONTROLLING CIVIL DISORDER

'Total freedom is anarchy; total order is tyranny' thus said Sir Robert Mark, when he was Commissioner of the Metropolitan Police in the 1970s. The right to strike, the right of peaceful persuasion on picket lines and the right to protest or demonstrate a point of view, are fundamental to liberal democracies, not only on moral grounds, but also for the practical reason that they provide a legitimate avenue for the pursuit of an objective and thereby reduce the likelihood of it being pursued by violent means.

Inevitably, all of these involve some disruption of community life, some obstruction and – especially on picket lines – some element of intimidation, all of which are technically breaches of the criminal law. The art of keeping the peace – as illustrated by England's record of having only 12 people killed in riots and demonstrations in 140 years (1843–1983) – is for the police to use their discretion in leaving some latitude for all of these criminal offences provided that they do not become excessive (as intimidation clearly did in the miners' strike in Britain in 1984) and, above all, provided that they do not escalate into violence, damage to property, injury and loss of life.

In these situations, some people will always be on the brink of such excesses and may deliberately push to the limit to provoke the police to overact or to see how far they can go. These people often arouse some disquiet even amongst their fellow strikers or demonstrators. The most effective deterrent is an awareness of the likelihood of being identified, arrested and convicted. Only thus will the right of the majority to picket or demonstrate peacefully be preserved.

The problem, which recurs in almost every context of violence examined in this book, is to balance the use of the available technology to keep the peace against the dangers of eroding civil liberties if those wielding the power of this technology abuse it. This balance must be maintained by public vigilance and this will come only if conflicts are fully and honestly reported in the media so that the public can recognize abuse when they see it, whether by police, pickets or demonstrators. The coming information explosion will make this easier but it will also provide channels for biased or selective reporting for propaganda or to arouse passions.

Developing technology will offer increasing facilities for identification of lawbreakers and the gathering of incontrovertible evidence for conviction. Not only will better, longer range photography in worse light be possible, but electronic aids for proving identity will become more widespread in the next ten years, whether or not Britain and the USA follow the majority of countries in introducing identity cards (see Chapter 6).

One of the lessons of the violent and intimidatory mass

picketing in the British miners' strike in 1984–85 was that a way must be found of protecting people against the evil of intimidatory mass picketing. The right to work must be protected as much as the right to strike, and the law grants immunity from civil damages only for what in police judgement (which can be challenged in the courts) is a reasonable number of pickets needed for peaceful persuasion. Even these are not immune from prosecution for breach of the criminal law – for example, obstruction, intimidation and violence. The miners' mass pickets, several hundred strong, attempting to push back the police cordon, to block the road physically against those going to work or driving vehicles, and to injure them (or the police) by throwing missiles, were clearly committing all three of these crimes, and this was witnessed publicly on television.

The police already have the power to turn people away from a picketed entrance if they judge that to increase the numbers would be likely to cause a breach of the peace. The general disgust at the violence and intimidation, shared by a majority of trade unionists, was such that the public will demand effective measures to prevent a recurrence and political parties will be under pressure to find solutions. One possible measure would be for the police to notify the union (or the strike leaders in an unofficial but lawful strike) of the numbers who will be permitted at each entrance to be picketed, and for this number of official pickets to be required to carry written authority from the striking union – possibly in the form of an official union card.

This, however, will at once raise a political or social problem. If the measures are so effective that strikes never succeed, the resulting frustration could lead to more and worse violence. This balance has had to be struck, and has usually been struck wisely with a great deal of police discretion, throughout the ebb and flow of industrial conflict since picketing was first legalized by Parliament in 1871. Ultimately the answer will lie in the growth of a desire within the trade unions themselves both to prevent violence and intimidation and to avoid their members earnings and, through damage to their industries, their long term prospects of earnings, being destroyed by strikes. It could be that the media coverage and consequent public outrage at the violence used by some of the miners in 1984 will help to advance the day when industrial disputes will be solved by argument before tribunals and courts – as they commonly are in Germany

– with union funds being spent on research and professional advocacy for these arguments rather than on strike pay and financing violent pickets. So the solution, like many others, will be social rather than technological.

Another controversial area is the degree of force which it is reasonable for the police to use to control the violence used against them by strikers, rioters and demonstrators. Over 1500 police were injured in the inner city riots in Britain in 1981 and many hundreds more in the miners' strike in 1984. When missiles, especially petrol bombs, are thrown, protective shields and visors are essential to reduce police injuries but the very appearance of these shields may raise the temperature. As violence escalates, the police should have call on a range of weapons with which to match it: truncheons, horses, dogs, water cannon, tear gas, plastic bullets and, in the last resort, firearms when firearms are used against them, as in Northern Ireland.

The tactics must be to avoid the use of any of these weapons, going up the scale only when absolutely essential, with the particular aim of containing the violence before firearms are used by either side. Thus far the British police have been remarkably successful in this respect. The last time firearms were used in a strike, riot or demonstration on the Island of Great Britain (as distinct from fighting armed criminals or terrorists) was in 1919, which was also the last time troops were called out to restore public order. If, however, in order to avert escalation to that level it becomes necessary for police to use any of the intermediate weapons (for instance, water cannon or tear gas) it is far better that they should be used by men trained rather than untrained in their use. This training does not mean that they will be used; the police had had access to tear gas for over 50 years before they used it for the first time in a riot in England in 1981. It must be hoped that it will be longer still before they have to use plastic bullets and they will never need to use lethal weapons at all in controlling public order.

Another kind of weapon which may justify further development is the incapacitating agent, which would cause temporary unconsciousness or disorientation without doing any lasting damage either to guilty or innocent people on the scene. This is further discussed in an anti-terrorist context in Chapter 5. There would again be problems of civil rights in controlling the use of such weapons but they could, in the end, prove to be the most humane anti-riot weapon of all.

One further problem may demand greater attention in the future. As the sinews of commerce and industry become growingly interdependent, these sinews, especially computer centres and communication networks, will become increasingly attractive as targets for disruption by demonstrators, rioters, intruders and terrorists. To deal with this, more active cooperation will be needed between the police and corporate security staffs. Companies cannot prevent crowds collecting or closing in on their premises; for this they must rely on the police. They can, however, make their premises and vulnerable points more secure; they can assist the police by maintaining good security and by being vigilant in their selection of personnel; in their procedures for identification and control of access; also in detecting indicators of disaffection or malice amongst their workforces. As with every form of security, the more manifestly effective their security, the less likely they are to be chosen as a target for disruption or attack. These security measures will be examined more fully in Chapter 8.

3   Terrorism and Terrorists

THE NATURE OF TERRORISM

Many convoluted definitions of terrorism have been coined. In essence, terrorism is the use or threat of violence against small numbers to put large numbers in fear; or, as well put by an ancient Chinese philosopher: 'kill one, frighten 10 000'. Criminal gangs apply this technique to dominate their districts and deter informers. Political terrorists use it to coerce officials and the public into doing things (or refraining from doing things) against their will.

There are also immediate by-products of terrorism which may sometimes be its primary aim, such as publicity, extorting of money and political blackmail. Publicity can be enormous: the PLO seized the attention of some 500 million (m) people when they kidnapped 11 Israeli athletes at the Munich Olympics in 1972; few people had heard of the South Moluccans until they hijacked a train in Holland in 1975; or of the Iranian Province of Khuzestan until six of its Arab inhabitants seized the Iranian Embassy in London in 1980. Huge ransoms have been extorted by political movements; for example, an estimated $240m by the Montoneros in Argentina in 1973–76. Nearly all the arrested Palestinian hijackers have been released by political blackmail exerted by further terrorist incidents.

Longer term dividends from political terrorism include destabilization by erosion of government confidence and public confidence, by exasperation and by provoking over-reaction. Very seldom, however, has it succeeded in actually overthrowing a government, especially a democratically elected government.

Guerrillas are not necessarily terrorists though they can

properly be so described when they use terrorism against the civilian population. When they kill one soldier they do not frighten 10 000 other soldiers – on the contrary, they spur them to greater efforts – but when they kill a civilian they do frighten thousands of others.

THE NATURE OF TERRORISTS

Political terrorists may be broadly subdivided by their motivation into nationalist, religious or ideological, though there is usually some overlap.

Nationalist terrorists, including secessionist and ethnic groups, are generally the most broadly based, with a substantial though not necessarily a majority popular base; examples of these are the Palestinians, the ETA in Spain, the IRA in Northern Ireland, the right-wing and left-wing guerrillas who use terrorist techniques in Central America. Their motivation often has ideological or religious overtones but in essence, it is to seize power over territory which they claim as theirs, whether they are in a majority or in a minority. Their loyalty is to a group or race rather than to an ideology or religion as such, though these may well be labels of identity. Their targets are usually governmental rather than commercial though they may use kidnapping or intimidation to extort money from local or expatriate commercial firms.

Religious terrorists are as old as religions. Most, in history, have acted in the name of one or other sect of Christianity or Islam (Buddhism has a clear record in this respect), but some have been inspired by other and sometimes more extreme or obscure religions. It is a paradox that, despite the moral principles of their religions, they are generally the cruellest and most fanatical of all terrorists towards both themselves and their victims. This has been illustrated in recent years by the ruthlessness of the Islamic fundamentalist killers sponsored from Libya and Iran, in some of whom the teachings of the Koran have been perverted to arouse a positive desire for martyrdom in the act of killing for their faith. The momentum of this fundamentalist philosophy, and its appeal to underprivileged Muslims who blame their plight on Western interference and Western values, is likely to increase in coming years. Western multinational companies and their expatriate and locally recruited staffs are likely to continue to be at risk, especially in Egypt and in the Gulf states where Khomeini has a following amongst both some of the students and poorer sections of the Arab community.

Ideological terrorists have motivations more diffuse and often harder to identify. They are found mainly in Europe and the Americas and come from both right and left. The ideology of right-wing terrorists (who sometimes borrow left-wing rhetoric) is not so much political as nationalist or racist and they come close behind the religious fanatics in their disregard of human life; though they have an educated leadership their appeal is mainly to poorer people seeking scapegoats (such as immigrants or intellectuals) for their plight and a wider group to which they can give their loyalty. Left-wing terrorists, by contrast, are recruited very largely from people who acquired their philosophy during higher education, and they are really a projection from the ranks of the protesters described in previous chapters. Some of them can be defined as 'issue groups' – examples of these are groups concentrating on a single issue such as computer technology (for instance CLODO in France) or animal rights (in Britain) or squatters rights (in several European countries) or nuclear power.

The development from peaceful protest to terrorism is a gradual one and only a very small number of protesters do in fact become terrorists. Most drop out, disgusted by the violence on the way. In West Germany in 1968–70 there were, perhaps, some 10 000 radical students who sympathized with the aims of the Baader–Meinhof group, but only about 50–100 of these graduated to the hard core of killers in the Red Army Faction (RAF) in 1975–77. The remainder had by then fallen out, either becoming more conservative in their views or directing their radical ideas into non-violent, legitimate – and more effective – activities such as journalism, teaching and the law. Those who did graduate to cold-blooded killing did so over the years in a process of escalation fuelled by frustration, as was described on pages 5–6. This process took some years and it is significant that none of the RAF killers were under 25 years old. That was probably because it does not come naturally even to human beings (in common with other mammals) to kill their own kind. It is very rare for a child, other than one deeply disturbed psychologically, to kill another child though the weapons (metal, glass, etc,) are easily to hand. The student protester, usually brought up in a sheltered home, graduates with unconscious reluctance through non-lethal violence and bombing to selective killing and the small hard core who do carry through as far as that may take five to seven years to do so.

It is not, in fact, inconsistent that PLO and IRA terrorists frequently kill at 18 or 20 years old. From earliest childhood they have been brought up to hate, Palestinians to hate the Jews, and Catholics in the slums of West Belfast to hate Protestants, 'Brits' and the police. In the areas of Northern Ireland where there is sectarian conflict (about ten per cent of the Province) the children go to different schools, the Catholics to their Church school and the Protestants to the state school. They never meet as friends or even as individuals – only as members of child gangs (*West Side Story* fashion) which hate and fight each other. By their early teens they are using knives, rocks and other missiles. By their late teens they are ready, in some cases eager, to kill. Even there it has been a five–seven year process.

STATE TERRORISM

State terrorism ('kill one; frighten 10 000') has historically been a weapon of the tyrant. It probably reached its peak in the Soviet Union under Stalin where even the most conservative estimates put the number of peasants killed to enforce collectivization at not less than 10m, some at 25m (mainly by calculated winter starvation). Hitler terrorized the Jews into submission. Gaddafi publicly hangs dissidents in Libya and sends gunmen to shoot down those who demonstrate their opposition whilst living or working in other countries. Khomeini, perhaps the most ruthless tyrant of the latter half of the 20th century, has killed tens of thousands of his people to quell opposition to his interpretation of Islamic law. Both Khomeini (by condoning the kidnapping of the entire US Embassy staff in 1979) and Gaddafi (by ordering his diplomats to shoot Libyan demonstrators in the streets of London from his Embassy windows in 1984) carried this to unprecedented lengths in flouting diplomatic conventions.

State terrorism in Latin America, the Caribbean and parts of

Africa takes more varied forms. Some governments follow Khomeini's pattern by using the police, the army and the judiciary to apply the terror quite openly. Others turn a blind eye to 'death squads' which murder political opponents and dissidents more clandestinely; in some cases these governments scarcely bother to conceal that many in the death squads are soldiers and policemen using their guns off duty. The public knowledge that there is an unlimited pool of them to draw from increases the terror.

DOMESTIC TERRORISM

The aims and motivations of internal domestic terrorists, nationalist, religious or ideological, were discussed earlier in this chapter. They can also be classified in relation to their sources of support.

Some groups, particularly in Latin America and Africa, are supported by a majority of their people in opposing an unwanted government in default of any democratic means of getting rid of it. These groups can be defined also as guerrillas, operating in either rural or urban areas, though they often also use terrorism as their tactic to deter collaboration with the government – as French resistance fighters did in 1940–45 to deter French people from collaborating with the Vichy Government and the Germans.

Other groups can claim the support of at least a substantial minority. About ten per cent of the Spanish Basque population support ETA and ten per cent of the Northern Irish population support Sinn Fein, the political front of the IRA.

In some cases, the support, whether of a majority or a minority, may be within a community largely resident outside the country, such as the Armenians and the Palestinians.

The more ideological terrorist groups, such as the RAF or the RZ (discussed later) in Germany, or the Red Brigades in Italy, usually have only a small supporting base amongst the population, almost entirely amongst students and graduates.

Other domestic movements may receive support from foreign governments, such as Iraq, Iran and Libya; also from the USSR, usually indirectly through Arab governments but sometimes more discreetly through the KGB based in the Soviet Embassy.

The IRA have received such support from the Libyan Government which undertook in 1984 to continue it.

Finally, domestic terrorist movements may receive support from overseas communities rather than from governments. The IRA receives support from NORAID, an Irish–American organization in the USA. ETA receives it not only from Spanish Basques living in France but also some, at least, from French Basques.

INTERNATIONAL TERRORISM

Between 1980 and 1982 the number of international terrorist incidents increased by 30 per cent, while the lethality in international and domestic incidents increased by 13 per cent between 1980 and 1983.

International terrorism may take the form of terrorist movements operating in other countries – Palestinians or Libyans in Britain and France or Iranians in Lebanon, Saudi Arabia and Kuwait; or of hijacking, kidnapping or killing people who are travelling or resident outside their own countries, whether the attack takes place in the home country of the terrorists (as often happens in Latin America), or in a third country (as often done by Palestinians or those acting on their behalf, such as Carlos in Paris and Vienna).

Terrorists operating outside their own country may aim to coerce a foreign government, or to intimidate their own nationals or refugees working abroad. Terrorists acting in their own country against foreign visitors or residents may (if the targets are diplomats) again be aiming to coerce governments or (if the targets are expatriate businessmen) to induce multi-national companies to pull out.

The last ten years have seen a substantial growth in one of these – the intimidation or murder of their own people in foreign countries or, to put it another way, fighting their battles on other people's streets. In London alone, the Bulgarians have killed a Bulgarian working for the BBC; militant Palestinians have killed conciliatory Palestinians and Israeli citizens; anti-Khomeini Iranian Arabs have seized Khomeini's Embassy; and, in April 1984, Gaddafi's diplomats fired from their Embassy window on anti-Gaddafi Libyans. Except in the latter case, when a British policewoman keeping the demonstrators away from the Embassy was killed, they have killed only each other.

The other recent development has been a new dimension in ruthlessness of terrorists towards both their victims and themselves, in the assassination of French and American diplomats and servicemen in Beirut and Kuwait in 1983 using huge explosive charges in trucks driven by suicidal terrorists. This dimension will be further discussed in the following chapters and in Part II.

4 Terrorism: Assessing the Threat in the Future

THE RISE AND DECLINE OF TERRORIST FASHIONS

Fashions in terrorism, such as the series of suicide truck bombs, rise and decline as unpredictably as other fashions. In 1968–73, for example, two fashions burgeoned and subsided: there was a rash of hijackings, averaging over 80 per year in 1969–70, which fell to a quarter of that number after 1973 when the USA led the way in the 100 per cent search of passengers and baggage at the boarding gates; and in Latin America there was a spate of kidnappings of ambassadors in 1968–70, which rapidly declined thanks largely to the heroic behaviour of Sir Geoffrey Jackson, the British Ambassador kidnapped in Uruguay in 1971. Thereafter, expatriate businessmen became the prime targets, especially in Argentina, where the ERP took $30m in ransoms in 1971–74 and the Montoneros takings reached $240m before they were broken by the military regime which came to power in 1976. Thereafter, while terrorism continued in Central America, the main focus of world attention switched to Europe, and especially to Germany and Italy, where assassination, maiming and kidnapping rose to a peak in 1977–78, after which both these countries introduced effective judicial, police and intelligence methods to break it. Concurrently, the army, police and intelligence services in Northern Ireland reduced the killing rate from 467 in 1972 to an annual average of less than 100 after 1977. The fashion then switched to the seizure of embassies with hostages, largely as a publicity venture. After an average of only three or four seizures per year from 1970–78, there were 35 in

1979 and 42 in 1980. Thereafter thanks to more effective protection and response, the number of seizures declined to 25 in 1981 and fell once again to a trickle after that.

In 1980–81, the amalgam of left-wing terrorists in El Salvador, the FMLN, conducted a massive fund-raising campaign by kidnapping expatriate executives of multinational companies. These had the secondary purpose of driving the companies out of the country. There were about 30 major kidnaps in 1980 of which 21 were for ransoms ranging from $80 000 to $1m. This income enabled the FMLN to launch and sustain civil war in which it is estimated that 40 000 people have been killed by the two sides, over 10 000 of them in each of the years 1980 and 1981. Thereafter, the exodus of people with money, expatriate and Salvadorean, and more effective government counter-measures, led the FMLN to switch their kidnaps for fund-raising to neighbouring Latin American countries. Meanwhile the civil war continued, though at a reduced intensity (the killing in 1982 fell to 5000). Kidnapping for ransom, however, remained high in Colombia and Guatemala.

The focus had meanwhile switched to the Islamic fundamentalist terrorism sponsored by Gaddafi and Khomeini. At the same time came a fashion for issue groups (anti-computer etc.) which began to proliferate in Europe, especially in France and Germany following the decline of the Red Army Faction in 1978–79; also, linked with these and with European protest movements, the 'diffuse' or 'undogmatic' guerrilla groups gathered momentum in Germany and this encouraged the appearance of similar groups in France, Italy and elsewhere in Western Europe. At the time of writing (1985), the Islamic fundamentalist and diffuse guerrilla philosophies are still in fashion with signs of continuing, so their tactics and techniques will be discussed more fully later in this chapter and in the next chapter.

The conclusion is that fashions rise and decline because terrorists seek vulnerable targets and techniques which achieve their aims (publicity, extortion etc.) but when these targets are removed or better protected, and when the response to the techniques of attack become more effective, the terrorists turn away to seek new targets and new techniques. The lessons for both governments and corporations are self-evident. They must look through terrorist eyes, watch for signs that new targets and techniques may become attractive and take effective action in time, both for protection and response.

The background against which to read these signs is the political stability of the countries in which incidents may occur and the effectiveness of the government and security forces in those countries.

INDICATORS OF STABILITY AND INSTABILITY

The prospects for political stability and violence in various countries of the world are analysed in Part II. There are, however, some indicators of general application, which may be used by government and corporate planners in assessing the security prospects of foreign countries in which they expect to operate.

Embassies have the task of maintaining statistical and qualitative information about the strength, organization, strategic aims and pattern of activity of political, dissident and terrorist movements in the country to which they are accredited; also of criminal gangs, large and small, and the patterns of crime; and about any links such movements or gangs have with each other, with politicians in or out of power, with sources of funds and with foreign governments.

Executives of multinational subsidiaries should be able to get such information from their Embassy staffs but should supplement this from sources of their own, which may be different from those of diplomatic or intelligence agents. It is extremely important to develop and maintain relationships with any such sources available, especially amongst those who have an interest in the continued operation of the subsidiary in their country.

Amongst the most important indicators are the economic ones; housing, living conditions, unemployment, inflation, shortages and the black economy; and generally whether the majority of the people seem to perceive a real hope of improvement in their standard of living and the security of their families under the regime in power; in other words, whether they have any deep-rooted incentive to maintain that regime and to support the preservation of order and stability.

Other indicators are to be found in the government and

bureaucracy – their efficiency, integrity and public standing; also in the police, the army and intelligence services – their political control, rivalries, efficiency, integrity, determination, public support and propensity to corruption.

Evidence of corruption is probably the most important indicator of all. A useful starting point is to find out how police pay scales and emoluments compare with the national average. If police pay is low and police recruiting is high, the conclusion is obvious.

Low-level corruption, for example, at police road checks or government licensing offices is the most easily detected and will almost invariably indicate more lucrative corruption at middle and higher levels, since the temptations and the size of the pickings will ensure that the disease grows all the way up the government promotion pyramids. Such corruption provides the enemies of the government (open, clandestine and violent) with their strongest justification for ousting it and with their strongest appeal for popular support in doing so.

Expatriate visitors and temporary residents may, however, often misinterpret corruption in some Third World countries due to a different system of taxation and of payment of government officials. As one Chinese put it to the author: 'in Europe money flows down; in Asia money flows up'. In Europe, taxes are collected into a central Treasury from which government salaries are paid and local projects financed. If this were attempted in many Third World countries it would not work, because the network of bureaucracy from state to province to district to village or precinct is too tenuous to implement such a centralized system; much of the revenue would remain uncollected, much of it would never reach the Treasury, and much of it would never get down the line to local officials, who would neither be paid nor receive the money with which to finance their local projects and services. Instead, therefore, the local official is given the authority to collect taxes, licence fees etc. in his district out of which he has to find his own salary, pay his staff, finance the local projects and services (country roads, water, medical etc.) and pay a stated amount, based on the population and economic activity of his district, to the next official up the line (for example, at the provincial level) who does likewise. If the district official fails to collect enough, either his services or his own salary will fall short. If, however, his total collections leave some to spare, he will probably keep the change. There is, of course, great scope for corruption in this system but it is the only system that will work in a country still building up a modern bureaucracy and the fact that an official operates under this system does not necessarily mean that he is corrupt. If he is, the system restrains him better than a more centralized system would. His people, who know the system, accept that he will take a reasonable income from it provided that it is not excessive and not at the expense of the services for which he is responsible. He may not be loved but he is tolerated.

The most disturbing indicator is evidence of large scale corruption at the top, which is endemic in many Third World countries and in some countries in Europe. Its commonest sources are: the sinecure ownership or chairmanship of large companies (especially of construction companies); non-accountable control of the distribution of commodities; and excessive 'commissions' from foreign and local companies with whom contracts are placed. Such people may not always reveal their corruption by an ostentatiously lavish lifestyle because they may well prefer to export their wealth to safe havens outside. If the people who hold supreme power have salted away large fortunes in foreign countries, this suggests that they have little confidence in their ability to solve their own country's problems, and only a limited incentive to do so. As soon as these problems seem to them to be getting out of control, they will turn their minds to picking the right moment to escape to their havens before the collapse comes. This can be the most deep-rooted and dangerous disease of all.

PROSPECTS IN AN UNSTABLE WORLD

The likely changes in the patterns of work and lifestyle in the 1990s, due to the microelectronic revolution, were described in Chapter 2 as a background to the prospects of industrial conflict and public disorder. Many of the same considerations apply to the prospects of terrorism.

While the main East–West balance is likely to be kept stable by nuclear sufficiency, the North–South relationship is likely to become more strained and internal conflicts in both European and Third World countries, as described in Chapter 2, are likely to increase.

In Western Europe, the Soviet Union will continue to use the KGB to exploit these conflicts, by discreetly providing material, propaganda, intelligence support and encouragement for both dissident and terrorist movements. The aim will be, not so much to further the political progress of these movements (because the USSR usually despises their politics and sees no realistic prospect that they will actually achieve any political power), but rather to destabilize Western societies and the structure of their economies and alliances.

The most disturbing trend amongst West European dissident and terrorist movements is probably that epitomized by the 'diffuse guerrilla' philosophy which is gaining ground in Germany. The organization and tactics of these groups will be taken as an example for discussion in the next chapter.

Right-wing terrorism in Europe is likely to be more sporadic but, when it occurs, more lethal and indiscriminate, as right-wing terrorists care less about public opinion.

The most dangerous movements of all in Europe and the Middle East will be the state sponsored terrorists directed by the Islamic fundamentalist regimes in Iran and Libya. The organization and tactics of the Khomeini's Shia terrorists are discussed in the next chapter. Khomeini's aim in sponsoring them is to drive Western influence out of the Islamic World, so they should be taken very seriously by both Western governments and Western corporations during the next few years.

Whatever the outcome of the Gulf war, neither Iraq nor Iran is likely to exercise more than limited influence in the area. If Iran prevails, Saudi Arabia and the other Gulf states will ensure that Khomeini's brand of Islamic fundamentalism will be prevented from spreading across the Arab world and will be supported in this by the USA and also by the USSR, which will be concerned about the effects on her own Muslim minorities. Similarly the Gulf states (supported in this case by the West but not the East) will limit the extension of Saddam's radical populist politics beyond the Iraqi borders. Such anomalies as the support of Iran both by Syria (against her old rival Iraq) and by Israel will continue, but there is no real prospect of a lasting resolution of the Arab–Israeli dispute or of the associated instability of Lebanon.

Pakistan has a history of political turmoil, arising both from political opposition to the military establishment and from resentment of minorities against domination by the 60 per cent Punjabi majority. The influx of 3m Afghan refugees into the North West Frontier Province and Baluchistan has not helped. Communal and religious strife seems to be endemic to all the four major countries of the sub-continent – India, Pakistan, Bangladesh and Sri Lanka – but, though this does regularly overflow into rioting and terrorism sometimes approaching civil war (as in the revolt of Tamils in Sri Lanka in 1983–84 and of militant Sikhs in India in 1984) expatriates and foreign companies are less likely to be targets than in most other countries.

In East and South East Asia, civil and guerrilla war is set to continue in Indochina owing to the attempts of Vietnam (supported by the USSR) to extend its influence and the determination of China to prevent this. North and South Korea have every logical incentive to resolve their differences but this still seems unlikely, so they will both probably continue to expand their economies but remain divided. Singapore and Malaysia will continue to lead the way to prosperity but the Philippines, for both geographical and political reasons, will remain unstable. So will the sprawling empire of Indonesia, which lags far behind its neighbours in both political and economic progress.

Southern Africa may still hope for a few more years of relative stability and economic growth, but West, Central and East Africa will remain subject to disturbance and foreign nationals and companies must always be prepared for a rapid deterioration in security or an overthrow of government in almost any of these countries.

Despite the intensity of the conflicts currently raging in Central America, the high level of kidnapping in Colombia and Guatemala, and the horrific debts of some of the South American countries, economic factors are likely to lead most Latin American countries towards a more stable period in the next, than in the past, ten years. There is, however, a disturbing development in Peru, where the Sendero Luminoso movement is attracting unprecedented support from the rural Indian community, harnessing the deep rooted Indian resentment of the rule of those of Spanish and Mestizo descent, whom they have historically regarded as foreign intruders in Inca territory.

This resentment now extends to foreign businesses in Peru, many of which have been attacked. The war is conducted with savagery on both sides with deaths rising steeply from 120 in 1982 to 1000 in 1983 and approaching 4000 in 1984. This violence seems likely to increase and could provide a model for imitation in other countries with large Indian communities such as Bolivia, Brazil, Guatemala and Mexico.

All of these areas are discussed more fully in Part II.

5 Terrorism: Trends in Technology and Tactics

TARGETS FOR TERRORISM

Year by year, as the microelectronics revolution unfolds, both manufacturing and service industries will become more interdependent and therefore more vulnerable to damage or disruption of crucial key points. In particular, as more businesses tie themselves in to computing centres, these will be seen as more effective points of attack by sabotage or bombing or disruption by 'moles' infiltrated into the centres. Since the cost of such damage will become greater, corporations may be more ready to pay ransoms to buy off a threat before the damage is done.

Disruption of computer communications and of other networks such as cable television will also be able to inflict increasing damage to business operations, with the same effects. There will be a constant race in research and development of means of tapping, intercepting and decoding data communications (whether by cable, fibre optics, microwave or other means) and of means to counter them. The dividends to be gained by establishing a mole or suborning a hitherto loyal member of staff will become even greater.

Human beings – staff and families – will become the most effective of all resources as targets for coercion, extortion and publicity. A corporation can write off a material asset worth millions of dollars at its face value but if it is seen to be callous about a single human life the effect on staff morale and public relations can be catastrophic. The various means of using people as pawns in the terrorist and criminal game are discussed later in this chapter.

Finally, each year sees more transport of toxic, explosive or flammable material, ranging from hydrogen cyanide and motor spirit to liquid natural gas and nuclear waste. Some of these are particularly vulnerable to hijack followed by the threat to ignite or discharge them.

WEAPONS: TECHNOLOGICAL DEVELOPMENTS

The hand-held personal weapon and the bomb are likely to remain the primary weapons of the terrorist. Certain trends in the design of personal weapons may prove to be significant during the coming ten years: the development of smaller weapons with higher rates of fire and higher penetration and lethality; the use of laser sights; and improving techniques for night vision. The first two will probably on balance help the terrorists; the third should on balance help protection against them.

There is already a weapon which can fire 25 rounds per second. It can be carried in a briefcase with a silencer and a laser sight which projects a bright orange laser dot onto the target. The firer has only to operate a trigger mechanism in the handle of his briefcase when the dot is on the heart of his target and six rounds should go through it in a quarter of a second, probably without him being suspected of possessing a weapon at all. The potential for the assassin, or for the indiscriminate killer firing on a crowd, is obvious. A prototype of this weapon is being developed with four barrels to fire 100 rounds per second, giving tremendous fire power to a single individual.

The development of caseless ammunition, in which the bullet is embedded in the propellant which burns up completely in the breech, removes the need to eject spent cartridges, enabling short bursts to be fired before the gun has time to kick. The Heckler and Koch G11, which came into service with the German army in 1985, embodies this principle, enabling it to put short bursts of three rounds in a very tight grouping at 300 yards range, greatly increasing lethality.

Other developments include hand guns which can penetrate body armour; area weapons which produce a shotgun effect with flechettes (needles) lethal at far greater ranges than shotgun pellets; miniature guns disguised as cameras for point blank firing (these may be totally free of metal and therefore particularly useful to hijackers); and weapons which can project small toxic pellets into the flesh, as with the 'hypodermic umbrella' used by Bulgarian intelligence officers to kill a defector in London but no longer requiring actual contact with the target.

For night vision, Infra-Red (IR), which 'illuminates' the target by projecting an invisible but still detectable beam, is being replaced by Thermal Imagery (TI) which projects nothing and is therefore not detectable, can see through smoke or rain, and whose pictures can be transmitted by the same microwave data link as transmits speech and stored data.

Hand-launched guided missiles capable of penetrating armour will certainly help the terrorist while being of little use to the soldier or policeman for fighting him. With such a weapon, it will be possible to destroy an armoured limousine from any fire position which gives a line of sight up to a mile away provided that the target is in view for long enough to launch and guide the missile to its target. Surface-to-air missiles – guided or heat-seeking – have already been used to shoot down civilian aircraft with heavy passenger casualities. Presumably the only reason why they have not been used more is the fear of adverse public reaction.

Parallel with the bigger car bombs with suicide drivers and remote control, a new dimension appeared in October 1984 – the precise long-delay fuse (as in video recorders). The IRA used one in their attempt to murder Mrs Thatcher in Brighton. Twelve more – destined for tourist hotels – were disclosed by good intelligence in July 1985.

It has been quite feasible for many years for terrorists to acquire the materials for a nuclear weapon and to assemble it; it is still easier for them to use devastating biological and chemical weapons. Though there have been about 70 hoax warnings on record, these weapons have not actually been used. The reasons for this are tactical or political rather than technical. Such operations would be more complicated than ones relying on guns or bombs, and so more likely to be detected; and the threat, in view of the enormous political price of carrying it out, would be less credible.

Much the same applies to the use of nerve gases which it would be quite possible for terrorists to acquire. They are, however, extremely difficult to control especially if there is any wind. Also, if they do work successfully, they cause such an indiscriminate and repulsive form of death that the main deterrent to their use is the odium and public outrage this would cause. For terrorist operations, guns and bombs are in any case more effective.

The development and tactical use of incapacitating weapons probably offers the greatest scope for change in the nature of terrorism and counter-terrorism. At present, tear gases cause only discomfort. Stun grenades daze and dazzle the victim for a few seconds only. Gases do exist which render the victim unconscious or disorientated without doing him any lasting damage but they take too long to act to be of much tactical use either to terrorists or to demonstrators or to the people combatting them. If an incapacitating gas were developed which took effect within a few seconds, it could add a new dimension to all these forms of conflict.

While technological development of weapons helps the terrorist, technological development of the means available for detecting him and for protection against him will clearly assist governments, corporations and the security of the public as a whole. The use of the technology already available, however, is restrained by political rather than technical considerations, notably by concern for the preservation of civil liberties, and this dilemma is likely to continue. It will be discussed more fully in Chapters 6 and 8.

LIKELY SOURCES OF VIOLENCE

The motivation for criminal violence will usually be monetary gain, but sometimes also revenge or intimidation of possible informers or rivals. Motivation of political terrorists will, in the long term, be the furtherance of a religious or political objective (examples of this are the overthrow of a government, independence, secession or the advancement of an ideology). To achieve these long term purposes, however, there will be immediate short term aims, such as publicity, political blackmail (for example release of prisoners), extortion of money, humiliating or discrediting a government or corporation, or coercing it to change its policies. It is these short term aims – the means to the end – on which security officers should focus their thinking in assessing terrorist risks and security against them.

The likeliest sources from which violence may come include criminals; disgruntled or dissident groups or individuals attempting arson or sabotage; demonstrators or rioters, motivated by political dissent, industrial conflict or social unrest; ideologically motivated terrorists, indigenous or international, left-wing, right-wing, environmentalist, nationalist or religious; domestic state terrorists, sponsored or condoned by their own governments in their own countries, overtly or covertly; international state terrorists operating outside their own countries and sponsored by their own or foreign governments (examples of these include the Libyan Government in Europe and the Iranian Government in Lebanon and Kuwait); and warring factions whose scale of fighting may range from guerrilla and terrorist actions to civil war (for instance in Lebanon since 1975) with whose conflicts expatriate organizations and individuals may get involved quite incidentally.

VIOLENCE AIMED PRIMARILY AT PROPERTY

Arson and sabotage will most often be carried out clandestinely by people who have penetrated or by-passed the processes of staff selection, vetting, identification, control of access or control of visitors, including labour employed by contractors doing work in the building; in other words, by people who are already inside, and whose malice is unsuspected. Once inside, it may be easy for them to do the deed and be outside the walls before the damage is detected or takes effect.

The growing scale and interdependence of data processing systems, including computers and communications, will make manufacturing and service industries and public service establishments more vulnerable to sabotage. There is scope for improving safeguards in the design of hardware and software to sound alarms or abort the intrusion of unauthorized material into the system. The main defence, however, must lie in vetting, identification and control of staff, visitors and contractual workers.

The rise in violent crime is likely to continue, demanding better protection by access control as above, and by secure perimeters and surveillance with instant reaction systems to impede escape once the alarm is tripped. These protective measures will be further discussed in Chapter 8.

Bombing has for many years been the most prevalent of all kinds of terrorist attack. The 1970s and 1980s have seen a rapid growth, accelerating in 1983–84, of the use of huge explosive charges in cars or trucks, occasionally driven by suicide drivers. Such bombs cause widespread and often indiscriminate casualties and for this reason they attract adverse public reaction over most of the world. They have been used less by the far left than by the far right – by religious fanatics or racialists or nationalists, such as the neo-fascists in Germany and Italy, Islamic fundamentalists, the IRA and ETA. This reflects a contempt for public opinion arising from the belief of religious or right-wing fanatics that, since they see themselves as representatives of their god or their race, they are justified in killing any who stand in their way. For two reasons this brand of terrorism must be expected to increase: because religious and racialist fundamentalism seems to have an increasing appeal, especially to those who believe or are persuaded that they are unfairly deprived; and because growing public familiarity with mass killings by terrorists means that still more outrageous shocks are needed to capture attention on television.

At the other end of the scale, the development of smaller, slimmer bombs with more sophisticated remote control for activation and detonation will make letter and parcel bombs more effective and harder to detect.

Hoax bomb calls are already highly disruptive (there were at one time as many as 40 per day in Northern Ireland, three per week to a single company). The trend is likely to be upwards, because anyone with loose change in his pocket can dial almost any number from anywhere in the world within a few seconds. This may be done as a mischievous impulse, so it is susceptible to fashions spread by media reports. More probably, however, it will aim to impose dislocation on a commercial organization at minimal risk. Telephone warnings, hoax or real, are usually very short, so tracing them will always be difficult, and this problem is further discussed in Chapter 8.

Blocking of access by demonstrators may prove increasingly attractive to anti-NATO or environmentalist movements in Europe against government and corporate targets, especially of installations connected with defence or the processing and storage of data. There is a tendency for such demonstrations to become more aggressive, partly because of the rising threshold of shock needed to attract media attention, and partly because, when peaceful demonstrations fail to achieve results, frustration usually leads to more violence. Second to that of seeking publicity, the likeliest aims of these demonstrations will be to disrupt the activities of defence, computer and multinational industries and to intimidate people from working for them.

Demonstrations may be used as cover by saboteurs, armed raiders or bombers to gain access to sensitive installations, with or without the connivance of the organizers of the demonstrations. This has been alleged, but not definitely proved, in relation to demonstrations in France and Germany against defence, computer and nuclear power industries.

Contamination and disruption of utilities (water, electric power, fuel, drainage, ventilation, heating and cooling, etc.) may prove an attractive tactic to the more ruthless kind of terrorists who now appear to be emerging, particularly those with the religious or racial convictions which engender a disregard for human life and for public opinion (such as those sponsored by the Iranian and Libyan Governments). Many such systems are very vulnerable and access to them is often less effectively protected than access to other more obvious key points. Infiltration of accomplices into either low grade jobs in the basements of buildings or into specialist maintenance and repair teams may offer relatively easy means of reconnaissance of the targets and the access, or of actually placing bombs or sabotaging machinery.

Long range weapons, with their improving accuracy and power of penetration of steel or concrete, may well become more fashionable for use by terrorists firing from the windows of buildings overlooking factories and office blocks, especially if they can locate key facilities (such as main switchboards or computing centres) which are close to outside walls.

Product extortion, by threat to pollute food, drink or

pharmaceutical products has increased substantially in recent years, largely due to the power of the media. The most lethal case on record, which cost at least seven lives, was the injection of cyanide into Tylenol tablets in USA in October 1982. This was done out of malice rather than for ransom, but it cost the parent company, Johnson and Johnson, tens of millions of dollars to rebuild confidence and recover their market share. A more typical pattern is that the head office of a food or drink chain receives a message saying that cans or jars injected with lethal poison and marked will be found on certain specified shelves. There is a demand for a ransom, and a warning that, if this is not paid, the shelves will be flooded with unmarked poisoned products and the mass media informed. Publication of such threats has on occasions cost supermarket chains millions of dollars in lost sales. Ezaki Glico, the Japanese confectionery manufacturer, is said to have lost $21 million in sales in May 1984 after a series of threats that packs of their sweets had been poisoned with cyanide, despite an attempt to pay a ransom of over $1m. If the extortioners are sensible enough to demand a ransom substantially lower than the potential losses there is a strong temptation to buy them off without revealing the threat to the police or to anyone else. This has no doubt been done on a number of occasions but generally, where there has been discreet cooperation between the company and an efficient and uncorrupt police force, the extortioners have either ceased to persevere with the threat or have been caught. Nevertheless, this form of extortion is likely to increase for two reasons: food, drink and pharmaceutical companies are particularly prone to amalgamation into large conglomerates and this will make them more vulnerable to the extortion of larger ransoms; and the proliferation of multi-channel sources of instant information into every home will make the threat of publication more effective.

Extortion by threat to do any of the above has historically been used by both criminals and political terrorists to raise money. In Malaya in the 1950s and currently in Spain and Northern Ireland, transport, hotel and other businesses have paid regular 'protection money' to buy off terrorists. In Latin America some multinational companies are believed to have paid seven figure sums in dollars to divert terrorists to other targets.

VIOLENCE AIMED PRIMARILY AT PERSONS

Personal attack and intimidation, especially of diplomats and expatriate executives, are likely to increase. The aims will be to force changes in government policy (as was achieved by Shia terrorists in Lebanon in 1983–84) or to drive out foreign-based companies (as was achieved by left-wing terrorists in Argentina in the 1970s and in Central America in the early 1980s). Methods of intimidation other than killing or wounding are sometimes used, such as the harrassment of families or malicious damage to cars and homes.

This tactic may be increasingly extended to intimidate locally recruited staff, to deter them from working for foreign organizations, or to suborn them into sabotage, betrayed of confidential information or collaboration with intruders or kidnappers. Such intimidation may be extremely hard to detect because a local staff member who has given years of loyal service and who still wishes to be loyal can be placed under intolerable pressure by threats to his family, to whom his loyalty will ultimately be greater. He will realize that to give even a hint that he is under coercion could place them at risk.

Kidnapping is a growing form of crime, generally for the extortion of a ransom, though there is sometimes an element of political blackmail; the examples include the release of prisoners or publication of a political manifesto. In Europe, especially in Italy, the majority of the victims have been citizens of the country, including children, and very seldom diplomats or expatriate business executives. The reverse has generally been the case in Latin America. Kidnapping for ransom, except within overseas Chinese communities, has been surprisingly rare elsewhere in the world.

Two different forms of kidnapping – short-term and long-term – require rather different responses. Short-term abduction has been prevalent in European countries and is usually carried out by criminals rather than political terrorists. Typically, a 'respectable' criminal gains access to a bank manager's office by posing as a client; the manager's telephone rings and his wife, in some agitation, says that gunmen have broken into their home and have taken her and the children hostage; and that unless he pays the man in his office £10 000 from the safe within ten minutes, the gunmen have threatened to shoot them or take them away to a secret location.

A short-term kidnap may thus become a long-term kidnap, in which the hostage is taken to an unknown location for days, weeks or months while a ransom is negotiated, usually by a series of short, sharp telephone calls. More commonly, however, a long-term kidnap begins with the abduction of the hostage from a car on the road between home and work or home and school. The first that the victim's firm or family hear of it is usually a telephone call from the kidnappers, demanding a ransom. This kind of kidnap may be done by either criminals or political terrorists and the response to it is discussed in Chapter 8.

There are a number of reasons why kidnap for ransom and other forms of extortion are likely to increase. Security of banks is constantly improving. The rapid supplanting of cash transactions by computerized credit transfers, and the payment of wages and salaries by bank credit, will result in a massive decline in the circulation, holding and transport of cash. It will, therefore, become easier to obtain money by extortion than by robbery.

Hostage seizure in a known location presents a problem totally different from that of a kidnap to a secret hideout because from the start it becomes a siege in which the police can deploy whatever force is necessary and they hold the initiative. The hostage-takers, therefore, have little hope of going free and the threat to kill their victims is weakened by the knowledge that if they do kill them all they will almost certainly die themselves. Their aim is, therefore, almost always to gain publicity so they will pick a newsworthy target such as an embassy, a computer centre, an oil refinery or a power station. Secondary aims may be to extort political concessions or simply to disrupt a key facility. If the target itself has sufficient bargaining potential (for example, by the threat of extensive pollution or fire) they may do without human hostages, but they will then get less publicity, less chance of extorting concessions and more chance of being killed if they resist capture.

There is no particular reason to expect hostage seizures and sieges to increase. As discussed in Chapter 4, the fashion will rise and decline with the success or failure of terrorists achieving their aims and their perception of their own chances of survival.

Hijacking is just another form of hostage seizure in which the aircraft, ship, train or coach are 'mobile premises' of a government or corporation. As happened in the TWA hijack from Athens to Beirut in June 1985, the passengers may be dispersed and held as kidnapped hostages. From 1972–84, improved airport security caused hijacking to decline but in 1985 this decline was reversed by a deterioration of security of which Athens airport was a notorious example, resulting in this spectacularly successful hijack, both in coercing governments and in attracting massive publicity, by Shia terrorists. Such success is likely to encourage more hijacking but it should also have the effect of goading airport authorities to tighten security, at pain of boycott by airlines and passengers if they fail to do so. As hijackers search for new ways of defeating search procedures the incident rate will rise and fall.

Extortion by threat to kill, maim or kidnap people can be even more effective than by threats against property. In the early 1970s, when kidnapping of executives in Argentina was at its peak, one multinational corporation paid $1m ransom in face of a threat that, unless they did so, one of their executives would be kidnapped. They had little confidence in Argentina's security forces, and they judged that the ransom paid for an actual kidnap would be higher than the protection money so they paid and were left unmolested. Fortunately for them, the terrorist movements in Argentina were destroyed soon afterwards following the 1976 military *coup*, before they could return for a second contribution (or a kidnap) from a corporation which had proved itself vulnerable.

EXAMPLE: THE SHIA TERRORISTS

Two of the very different kinds of terrorist tactics which have recently emerged merit a careful watch over the coming years as they have proved more than usually successful and may therefore persist and be imitated. These are the tactics of the Shia terrorists seen in Lebanon and the Gulf and the tactics of the 'diffuse guerrillas' in Germany.

The Shia terrorists have been built round some 1000–1500 Iranian Revolutionary Guards sent by Khomeini in 1983 to operate in Lebanon from a Syrian army base in the Beka'a

Valley. They have trained and motivated other Shia groups in Lebanon (which has a 30 per cent Shia minority) and in the Gulf states. The main characteristic of these Shia terrorists, including the Iranian Revolutionary Guards, is that they are indoctrinated with a fanatical faith which engenders ruthlessness in taking lives and a belief that martyrdom will take them to eternal paradise. This fanaticism has been very apparent in the internal conflicts and executions inside Iran itself since 1979.

Most of the Shia terrorist operations (usually mounted under the war name Islamic *Jihad*) have been small scale ambushes in the fighting in Lebanon, using small arms or remotely controlled mines but, in the 12 months from April 1983, there were 22 major vehicle bomb attacks. Five of the vehicles (four in Lebanon, one in Kuwait) were driven by suicide drivers and killed more than 400 people, including 290 Americans and 60 French. It was seen as a direct result of these attacks the Multinational Force of British, French, Italian and US contingents was withdrawn from Lebanon enabling Syria, one of Iran's few Arab allies, to establish control over the Lebanese Government and all the territory of Lebanon other than that occupied by Israel.

This was a major success for state-sponsored terrorism. It also demonstrated a degree of logistic organization which could only have been achieved with large scale backing by one or more governments (in this case, of Iran and Syria). The suicide attack on the US Embassy in Kuwait on 12th December 1983, for example, was one of 11 attacks in that country on the same day. It is also significant that all five suicide truck bomb attacks were on expatriate targets, two of them on embassies.

In view of its political success, this use of truck bombs may be repeated by other governments and right-wing, nationalist or religious movements which feel themselves to be morally justified in mass killing for their faith or ideology. Remote control of firing by radio is already used and, since the use of suicide drivers expends the lives of the most dedicated men they may turn to remotely controlled locomotion for the final stages of the approach, enabling the driver to get away. Prime targets for such attacks will be Western embassies and Western multinational establishments, both in the Middle East and in Europe, aimed at driving Western influence out of Muslim countries and Israel.

EXAMPLE: THE GERMAN 'DIFFUSE' GUERRILLAS

The tactics of terrorism and disruption which have developed in Germany since 1977 have established a totally new trend whose effectiveness may lead to it being imitated elsewhere in Europe. This is the combination of 'diffuse' or 'undogmatic' guerrilla groups with anti-NATO, anti-nuclear, anti-computer and environmentalist demonstrators.

The principal diffuse groups are the Revolutionary Cells and their female cousins in Red Zora, which are known by the same acronym, RZ. They were responsible for most of the 400 bombing and arson attacks in Germany in 1983 but, learning from the failure and declining support of the Red Army Faction (RAF) they attack property rather than people, and generally do their bombing in the silent hours (2–4 am) to avoid killing people. They do sometimes maim politicians, judges, officials, etc. as a 'punishment', and have on occasions killed them 'by accident', but generally they avoid doing so because they know that it alienates the young and idealistic people in the ranks of the environmentalist groups and other demonstrators whose sympathy they hope to attract.

The RZ consists of a number of autonomous cells, each three–eight strong, with no central direction. They are part-time terrorists, living at home, so they need no safe houses, few communications and little logistic organization. This makes them difficult to penetrate or catch.

They are guided by a philosophy rather than a strategic plan: to discredit and undermine the German democratic system; to harass the defence industry, NATO and the deployment of US nuclear missiles; to impede the pollution of the environment by nuclear power, extension of roads and airports and microelectronics ('psychological pollution'); and to demonstrate disapproval of multinational companies in Germany and in the Third World and of US foreign policy, especially in Europe and Central America. They link their activities to the existing mass protest movements about these things in the hope of widening their popular base and arousing public opinion.

Within these parameters, the individual cells have complete freedom of action striking when and where the spirit moves them, which makes it difficult to predict their targets. This is also the philosophy of other 'diffuse' movements such as the Autonomists and the Anti-Imperialists. Despite some Marxist rhetoric, they are closer to anarchism than to organized Leninism. As well as bombing they have cooperated with demonstrators invading computer centres and destroying computer data. They have also used some original propaganda techniques: for example, they seized a local radio station and broadcast 'black propaganda' which was plausible enough for listeners to think it was authentic; and they have secured the publication in a reputable newspaper of a detailed guide on how to sabotage computers. The overall purpose is the destabilization of Germany's very successful society.

The German police and intelligence services have developed efficient means of countering lethal terrorism but they have not succeeded in getting their hands round these autonomous cells. Working in concert with the demonstrators, they are seen as achieving results where the RAF's lethal terrorism failed, so they may prosper and be imitated in Europe and elsewhere in the Western world.

To sum up: fashions in terrorism rise and decline according to their success or failure. Developing technology will make certain targets, notably those dependent on computers and communications, more vulnerable. Weapon development will generally increase the powers of the terrorist while that of electronic and other surveillance techniques, in so far as they can be applied without unacceptably infringing civil liberties, should help protection against them. Improved security and declining circulation of cash will make extortion relatively more attractive than robbery. And those whose security is manifestly the best are unlikely to be selected as targets. All of these matters are further discussed in Chapters 6, 7 and 8.

6 Security and Civil Rights in a Liberal Society

THE FUNDAMENTAL DILEMMA

It is a paradox that, in protecting a society from violence or coercion, it may be inevitable on occasions to restrict civil liberties in order to preserve them. This is accepted by the majority, indeed by an overwhelming majority if the violence is lethal. Violent demonstrations in democratic societies are disliked, and terrorism is detested.

One of the commonest tactics of political violence is to make liberal judicial procedures unworkable by intimidating witnesses and juries so that, in order to maintain the rule of law, it becomes necessary to turn to less liberal judicial procedures. In both Northern and Southern Ireland, for example, governments of all parties have had to suspend trial by jury for terrorist offences as the systematic murder and intimidation of witnesses and jurors made it unworkable. The Germans have had to control prison visits by lawyers to prisoners awaiting trial for terrorist offences and to install glass panels between these lawyers and their clients because the lawyers were abusing their professional code to smuggle weapons and to act as couriers between the prisoners and their terrorist organizations outside. There is also provision for excluding a lawyer from a trial if there are good grounds suspecting that he was involved in the crime of the defendant. In Italy, judges have the power to detain an accused person indefinitely if his accomplices prevent his trial from proceeding by intimidation of witnesses or jurors. All of these measures, introduced in the face of murder and intimidation, were supported by a large majority of the public in their countries.

The dilemma is that, if such restrictions are greater than the situation appears to the public to justify, or if they cause excessive inconvenience or harassment to innocent people, the essential public support may be lost.

The ultimate civil right, however, is the right to live. A violent minority, whatever its politics, has no right to kill, and no claim to such a right must ever be allowed to override the right of the majority to live in peace. One of the arts of governing a liberal society is to ensure that the public understands and approves of the measures which are necessary to preserve this principle. A basis for that approval is to establish clearly that the government stands for stability, and the rule of law while the terrorists stand for disruption and the rule of fear.

CONTROL OF ARMS AND EXPLOSIVES

By far the most important measure for public security against political violence and violent crime is the effective control of firearms, ammunition and explosives. In some countries, the state of security may be such that certain people, such as isolated farmers in remote areas, have to be licensed to carry guns for protection of their families but the granting of these licences should be kept to a minimum. A gun in the hands of someone not fully trained and, equally important, not psychologically prepared to take the instant decision whether or not to use it, is in fact likely to increase the danger of him being shot by an armed intruder or kidnapper. In an ideal society, the bearing of arms should be the monopoly of the police and armed forces, and they should only carry them when there is a real likelihood of them being attacked by armed criminals, invaders or terrorists.

It is particularly desirable that police handling demonstrations should be unarmed. Britain is one of the few large industrial countries where this is so and, as a result, less than 12 people have been killed in riots, demonstrations and strikes in England, Scotland and Wales in the whole of the 20th Century. In Northern Ireland, where illegal possessions of arms by both the rival comunities has made it inevitable for the police also to carry arms, the picture has been very different. If weapons had not been used in the initial outbreaks of rioting in

1969, the situation would probably never have escalated into terrorism.

There should be very severe penalties for the unauthorized possession of arms, ammunition or explosives, and their registration should be strictly enforced. In countries where, for historical reasons, it has become customary for citizens to possess guns (as in the USA, where the right to do so is enshrined in the Constitution) the homicide rate is always high because the knowledge that every security guard and many householders are armed leads many more criminals to carry arms and, when cornered, to use them. This means that the police, too, are also quick to draw their guns. Since the use of guns becomes commonplace, people are more likely to use them for political terrorism too. The more they are used, the more people carry them, legally or illegally, and there is a vicious spiral.

The possession and use of other weapons which can injure, kill or destroy property is more difficult to control. Some, like knives, chisels or bottles, may be carried for plausibly legitimate purposes. Others, like petrol bombs, leave no doubt about their purpose, to burn, injure or kill; so their possession and their use should carry penalties comparable with those of possessing or using guns. Petrol bombs are both indiscriminate and vicious; they should be regarded as a form of napalm because, like napalm, their liquid content is calculated to sink into or stick to clothing or skin and thereby to inflict serious burns.

Bulk explosives are difficult to control because they can so easily be improvised (from certain kinds of fertilizers and diesel fuel) but they cannot be fired without the use of detonating and priming charges (such as plastic explosive) which it is difficult and dangerous to manufacture outside a factory. It should therefore be practicable to control the manufacture of detonators and high explosives, and to enforce strict accounting into and within the quarries and mines which are licensed to use them.

Nevertheless, the size and quantity of detonators and plastic explosive needed to fire a truckload of bulk explosive are very small and easy to smuggle, so control would be greatly enhanced if they were required by law to be tagged during manufacture with material which can be reliably detected by screening equipment. This, however, would only be really effective if all or, at least, most of the world's governments subscribed to it. There are unfortunately a large number of governments which would not do this, or would permit or organize the manufacture of untagged detonators and explosives on the grounds that they should be available to 'freedom fighters' for justifiable use in 'wars of liberation'. This justification is claimed by most Communist countries and many Middle Eastern, African, Caribbean and Latin American countries. This claim is also used to negate effective international action in relation to extradition of terrorists, abuse of diplomatic bags for smuggling weapons, as discussed elsewhere in this book.

As with almost all anti-terrorist measures, the most effective security against improper possession and use of firearms and explosives comes from a good intelligence system.

INTELLIGENCE SERVICES

In a liberal society it is extremely easy to use a gun or a bomb to kill or destroy (even if not always so easy to escape after doing so). Excessive crime and terrorism will provoke alarm and a public clamour for restriction of civil liberties such as freedom of movement and privacy, so the bulwark for maintaining a free society lies in a good intelligence system which can detect those who abuse its freedoms to kill or destroy before they can do so, and to make their arrest and conviction so likely that others will be deterred.

Though technological developments can help (for example, night vision and surveillance devices) anti-terrorist intelligence depends primarily on human intelligence provided by informants handled by professional intelligence officers. Penetrating criminal or terrorist organizations is very difficult because they usually take stringent precautions to prevent it, such as long probationary periods before new recruits are accepted, investigation of personal background, the maintenance of a credible threat of retribution against friends or relatives, and sometimes a requirement to prove commitment (for instance, 'kill a cop').

Very occasionally a spectacular mole has been infiltrated into an extremist political movement (the Secretary-General of the Malayan Communist Party from the late 1930s to 1947 was a

British Special Branch agent) but success has much more often come from 'turning' someone already in or close to the movement or gang – persuading him or her to stay with them, for example, or maintain contact with them but at the same time getting them to act as a police informer, usually encouraged by a substantial reward. A lesser version of this is to persuade someone after arrest to put the finger on others and to give evidence as a witness for the prosecution against them in exchange for immunity or leniency. This has been done with particular success by the police in Northern Ireland and Italy.

Recruiting such informants, whether before or after the crime, is generally achieved by presenting them with an array of evidence which leaves no doubt that, for them at least, the game is up. To achieve this, there is no substitute for a good intelligence system, but every possible means must be used to prevent it from being used improperly in such a way as to prejudice civil liberties, especially of innocent people.

Intelligence services must inevitably operate secretly, and must record information about individuals, so it is essential that they are strictly monitored and strictly accountable. This will become even more important as the development of micro technology leads to the recording of more and more personal data, not only by intelligence services but also by other government departments, by banks, by retail organizations and by anyone else whose business uses computerized credit cards.

The balancing act of securing the potential benefit of micro-electronic technology to prevent murder and malicious damage and at the same time restricting the power which this technology will put into the hands of those who control it poses a dilemma which has not yet been solved and will become increasingly difficult to solve as the technology develops.

How is it possible to monitor a secret intelligence service and at the same time preserve the confidentiality without which it cannot be effective? If the faces of the intelligence officers who handle the informants become known by the criminals or political terrorist movements, then the informants themselves will be at risk of being killed or threatened, so other informants will be intimidated and the flow of information will dry up.

This was the cardinal error made by the Italian Government in their emasculation of their own intelligence capability in 1976. First, they dismissed a number of the top directors of the intelligence services who were suspected of abusing their positions by using intelligence information to smear or coerce left-wing politicians. There were good grounds for this suspicion in some cases, but the Government failed to replace them with any effective new management, so the prestige and morale of the intelligence services was shattered, the more so because they were still expected to do a highly dangerous job. To make matters worse, the Government introduced a law that any examining magistrate investigating a case had the right of access to the intelligence file of any person involved in the investigation. This meant that a criminal or political terrorist had only to get one of his friends to persuade a gullible or corrupt magistrate to ask for his file and he could soon be reading it himself.

A police or intelligence informer giving really valuable information will generally be someone who knows the person he is giving information about and is therefore probably known by that person. It follows that even if the informer is not named on the file, the person informed against will usually be able to guess from the nature of that information where it came from. This is what happened in Italy, and the violent retribution which followed quickly deterred others, because no-one would give sensitive information about a criminal or terrorist if he knew that the subject was likely to have access to it. The almost total drying up of information resulted in a field day for both criminal gangs and Red Brigades (BR) terrorists, and the number of criminal and political kidnappings, in particular, reached record levels in 1977 and 1978. The climax came when Aldo Moro, ex-Prime Minister and potential President, was kidnapped, held undetected in Rome for six weeks and then murdered.

Chastened, the Italian Government rebuilt an effective intelligence organization and gave it the power of appeal against a magistrate's request for access to a file, an appeal which could be overruled only by a Cabinet Committee headed by the Prime Minister and the Minister of the Interior. This was part of a comprehensive package of anti-terrorist laws introduced in 1980. Almost at once, both crime and political terrorism decreased and the arrest rate accelerated, culminating in a highly successful intelligence operation leading to the rescue of the kidnapped American General Dozier in January 1982. This operation led to a further flood of intelligence, including the seizure of 25 BR hideouts containing documents and other evidence. Several hundred BR terrorists and supporters were arrested including many of the leaders. In January 1983 the surviving leadership announced that BR had abandoned the armed struggle and, though some of its more militant members have dissented and will no doubt continue to do so, the number of political terrorist murders has fallen from 135 in 1980 to 27 in 1982 and only three in 1983. There could be no more convincing proof that good intelligence saves lives.

The Germans proved the same point by a radical reorganization of their police intelligence system after the arrest and murder of Dr Hanns-Martin Schleyer in 1977, notably by improving the computerized storage and classification of data. As a result the RAF has been kept on the run, having to devote almost all its efforts to survival and there have been no RAF murders (despite two attempts which failed) nor any successful major operations from 1977 until 1985.

The Germans have also demonstrated the best way to monitor an intelligence organization. The directors of their main intelligence services – BND (international), BFV (constitutional) and BKA (criminal) – are all publicly named and subject to parliamentary and press scrutiny. So are their senior executives. They work in normal government offices with no more than the normal degree of security of access necessary for any sensitive establishment. The intelligence officers on the ground, however, who are in direct contact with the informants, operate in complete secrecy, are known only to those who need to know, and are answerable only to their superior officers in the service unless they actually break the law. This is as it should be. The directors and senior executives are fully and publicly accountable for the actions of their subordinates. Like any other civil servants in a democracy they are responsible to their minister who is in turn responsible to Parliament. If his civil servants are criticized the Minister can back them or sack them or take the blame himself and resign.

One problem remains: how can the directors be monitored and explain their actions without revealing secrets which could prejudice security? There are three alternative bodies in a democracy which can be made responsible for monitoring: the executive, the legislative or the judiciary. It is clearly not satisfactory for the executive to monitor an intelligence service responsible to itself. The problem with committees of the legislative is that they will contain representatives of all parties and some of these may have political aims which would inhibit frankness by officials in discussing sensitive matters. A committee of the judiciary, provided that it is genuinely independent, is probably the best. Obviously its examination of officials must be confidential, but democracy must in the end depend on a degree of trust, and if the people cannot trust the executive or the legislature or the judiciary, it is hard to imagine how a democracy can function at all.

RECORDING AND STORAGE OF INTELLIGENCE DATA

An equally difficult and sensitive dilemma arises over the recording and use of personal data and other intelligence information. The use of a computer system for its storage and retrieval is vastly more efficient than the now outdated filing and card index systems. During the six weeks of Dr Hanns-Martin-Schleyer's kidnap, the German police were on two occasions only one day too late in locating the hideouts where he was held in Germany before he was moved on to Belgium, Holland and France. The German public, outraged by the kidnap, had flooded the police with 3826 pieces of information. One of these seemed of no particular significance but if it had been recorded on a computer instead of in a paper file it would have automatically been linked with another of the 3826, which would have led the police to his second hideout in time to rescue him but they did not spot the link until it was just too late. The computer could have saved Schleyer's life and those of other RAF victims before him. This prompted the Government to authorize the police to install the expensive nationwide computerized surveillance and intelligence system (the BEFA) which prevented the RAF and other movements from carrying out any successful major operations from 1977–84 and also helped to apprehend many other criminals.

The problem is that, while such a system is highly effective in protecting the lives of the public against terrorism and crime, it is very difficult to make watertight provisions against it being improperly (or just stupidly) used to prejudice the civil liberty of an innocent individual. While tight regulations can be made to prevent any *official* release of information (for example, by the police to a potential employer anxious to check the reliability of someone applying for a job) it is virtually impossible to prevent an irresponsible or misguided official from revealing a damaging piece of information in a private conversation, directly or through a friend – for instance that the individual is alleged to have been seen in the company of a known criminal or political extremist or to have been involved in a fraud, both of which might be quite unsubstantiated. There is no easy answer to this unless future technological development produces a really reliable lie detector – which would, of course, have far wider implications than just this one. For the time being this, like many other civil liberties, must depend ultimately on trust, on the integrity of those with access to power over the liberty of others. This in turn depends on meticulous selection of such people, strict supervision, and severe punishment if they betray their trust. The answer, however, does *not* lie in removing the far more important protection which an efficient intelligence system offers to the majority of the community – the right to live – which depends upon detecting and stopping the tiny minority who claim the right to kill for political or criminal gain.

IDENTITY CARDS

The controversy over identity cards has many similarities. In the majority of industrialized countries they are compulsory; in every country, people working in any sensitive establishment, government, industrial or commercial, will be required to carry one. A growing number of people voluntarily carry credit cards, banker cards etc. Almost all of these cards, obligatory or voluntary, now carry an increasing amount of electronically recorded magnetic data to guard against forging a card or impersonating the holder. If the full potential capability of developing technology is used, such forgery and impersonation will become very difficult. This should be wholly beneficial to the community. The abuse of such information is restrained by proper public concern about it, but opposition to its development is sometimes emotional rather than rational, except amongst those who wish to have a free rein in pursuit of a malicious purpose. With reasonable safeguards against abuse, people going about innocent business or pleasure should have little to fear and much to gain from the prevention of fraudulent access or impersonation.

The processes and potential development of access control and prevention of impersonation are further discussed in the context of selection and vetting of personnel and security of premises in Chapter 8.

EMERGENCY LEGISLATION

The introduction of compulsory identity cards (where not already required) is one of the contingency plans which every government should have in readiness in case of a sudden emergency or escalation of terrorism. There are many other things which these contingency plans should cover – for example, stricter registration of lodging and residence (already in force in many countries such as the Netherlands), and authority for the police to tap telephones in emergency with retrospective approval or reversal by a judge within a specified time (in force in Italy since 1980 to facilitate quick and effective response to kidnapping).

The British Government clearly had contingency legislation ready in draft in 1974, when a sudden upsurge of IRA bombing led to the passing of the Prevention of Terrorism Act. Because it had been thought out in advance of the crisis, it was possible to take it through all its stages quickly and it became law within a week. It imposed control on all movement between Northern and Southern Ireland and Great Britain, extended the length of time for which suspects could be held for investigation, made the collection or donation of funds to support terrorist movements illegal, and various other measures. All of these were designed directly or indirectly to assist the police in obtaining intelligence to prevent terrorist murders. In this respect they were very successful. In 1974, 40 people had been killed by the IRA in England, but only nine were killed in 1975, one in 1976 and none in 1977. The numbers killed have remained low ever since, as many by Arabs as by the IRA, but enough to make it necessary to renew the Act each year. As in Italy and Germany, better intelligence has saved lives.

PROTECTION

Physical protection against violent demonstrators, rioters, criminals and terrorists is a task which falls upon government departments, corporations, families and individuals alike. The techniques involved and the likely potential for technological development of these are much the same for whichever is doing them so their examination will be deferred until Chapter 8. This will include protection of premises, facilities, transport and personnel against the various forms of attack which were discussed in Chapter 5.

7 Government Response: Coordination and Control

INTERNATIONAL COOPERATION

International cooperation against terrorism amongst the world community as a whole has been largely ineffective because too many countries have been willing to use terrorism, or at least to support it, overtly or covertly, as a tool of foreign policy. This includes notably the Soviet Union, Cuba, Iran, Iraq and Libya but also many other Arab countries (even if only unwillingly paying protection money) who have provided funds and facilities used by the PLO for international terrorist operations; also large numbers of African countries, not only in Southern Africa but, in the guise of supporting 'wars of national liberation', in any neighbouring African country they wish to destabilize. The same applies to a lesser extent in the rest of Latin America and Asia. Indeed, if one were to class the tactics of the Second World War resistance fighters against their fellow-countrymen who collaborated with the occupation forces as terrorism (and strictly speaking they were because their aim, however justifiable, was to terrify others who might be induced to collaborate) then very few countries in the world could claim never to have supported terrorists of one kind or another during the past half century.

Since, therefore, the difference between a terrorist and a freedom fighter lies in the eye of the beholder, the United Nations has never reached any satisfactory definition of a terrorist. Also, no matter how inhuman the actual crime, for example, kidnapping or murder of children, or indiscriminate bombing of innocent bystanders, very few countries will extradite even the known perpetrator of such a crime if he can establish a claim that the motivation of his action was political.

For all these reasons, UN Conventions or Resolutions on the subject have been virtually useless and the same has applied to almost every attempt by any group spanning either the East–West or the North–South divide. One of the relatively more effective attempts was by the Council of Europe (21 countries) in the European Convention on the Suppression of Terrorism in 1977. The original draft (Article 1) specifically excluded certain offences from being classed as political offences for purposes of extradition, including aircraft hijacking, attack on diplomats, hostage-taking or the use of bombs 'endangering persons'. Unfortunately, however, this was made useless by Article 13 which empowered any signatory to 'declare that it reserves the right to refuse extradition in respect of any offence mentioned in Article 1 which it considers to be a political offence . . .'. There were various other loopholes (for example, no obligation to extradite 'if the requested state has substantial reasons for believing that the request for extradition . . . had been made for the purposes of prosecuting or punishing a person on account of his race, religion, nationality or political opinion, or that that person's position may be prejudiced for any of these reasons' (Article 5). These loopholes were left in the hope that all 21 members would sign the Convention but even so three declined to sign it and the majority of the rest have still not ratified it.

At a meeting in Bonn in July 1978 the seven countries of the 'Economic Summit' (Canada, France, Germany, Italy, Japan, UK and USA), agreed to extradite or prosecute anyone who had hijacked an aircraft landing on their territory; moreover, they undertook to refuse to allow the landing of any aircraft operated by or coming from any country which failed to extradite or prosecute a hijacker, and to cut off that country from their own air traffic. This, on paper, was a powerful agreement as these seven countries between them operated 80 per cent of the free world's commercial air traffic, and its deterrent effect probably has contributed to the decline in hijacking. It still, however, has one decisive weakness: an undertaking to prosecute can never be an undertaking to convict. If the country holding the hijacker wished for any reason not to extradite him, it could get out of it by prosecuting and then acquitting him. In practice, even these seven summit countries themselves are unlikely to extradite a hijacker if to do so would seriously prejudice their national interest, (for instance, to extradite an Arab hijacker to Israel whilst engaged in a delicate and important political or commercial negotiation with an Arab country). National self-interest will, sadly, remain the ultimate consideration so long as there is no binding system of international law under a supranational body with real power to enforce it, and there is no prospect whatever of this coming about.

The same limitation applied to the agreements by the same seven countries at the London Economic Summit in June 1984, which particularly focused on the problems of state-supported terrorism carried out by people with diplomatic status, using weapons smuggled in diplomatic bags. The seven countries pledged closer cooperation between police and security organizations in the exchange of information, intelligence and technical data. This was the most promising part of the agreement because, if governments give their police and intelligence organizations the authority and the means to cooperate, they will take every chance of doing so, as fellow professionals glad to be free of political restraints in fighting a common enemy. The effectiveness of other parts of the 1984 Economic Summit declaration will, however, depend on the will of the governments to enforce them, which in turn will depend on their seeing long term self-interest in enforcing them rather than weakening them for reasons of short term political expediency. They pledged to scrutinize their own laws to remove loopholes, to exercise stricter control of the size and range of diplomatic missions enjoying diplomatic immunity, to review the sale of weapons to states which supported terrorism and to consult and 'as far as possible cooperate' over expulsion and exclusion of known terrorists including individuals with diplomatic status.

This declaration came in the wake of a series of violations of the 1961 Vienna Convention on diplomatic immunity by certain countries, notoriously Iraq, Iran and Libya. The Iranian Government created a new precedent in flouting both the Vienna Convention and civilized standards of behaviour when they condoned and then supported the seizure of the US Embassy and of its entire staff as hostages for 444 days in Tehran in 1979–81. The Libyan Government also has abused diplomatic privilege on many occasions, using the diplomatic bag to smuggle weapons with which to kill anti-Gaddafi Libyans in European countries. The most flagrant case was in April 1984 when one, or more probably two, Libyans with diplomatic immunity fired from the windows of the Libyan Embassy in London at a group of anti-Gaddafi Libyan demonstrators, wounding 11 of them and killing a British policewoman who was one of those keeping the demonstrators away from the Embassy across the street. Britain and the USA, with commercial activities worldwide, have an interest in observing the Vienna Convention, and have little answer to those who do not, other than to break off diplomatic relations and expel their diplomats, and this was done on that occasion. The British public was, however, outraged to watch on television as the known murderers were escorted out of the Libyan Embassy to be flown to Libya and still more so when large packages, obviously containing the guns used for the murder, were loaded to accompany them as 'diplomatic bags'.

In fact, it was later admitted that the British authorities could have opened and examined these and all other Libyan diplomatic bags had they chosen to do so because Gaddafi had expressly reserved the right to search any diplomatic bags entering or leaving Libya, and the British Government had consequently declared the same right in relation to Libyan diplomatic bags. Nevertheless, the British Government were wise not to exercise this right, nor to arrest the diplomats believed to have fired the shots. It is better to maintain diplomatic relations only with countries which are willing to sign and respect the full provisions of the Vienna Convention, and it would be unwise to amend the Convention to accommodate governments which openly use kidnap and murder in the diplomatic process.

One line of approach worth pursuing would be for the majority of the countries of the world to agree to submit their diplomatic bags for X-ray at the point of entry, and to announce that they would require all diplomatic bags entering their countries to be similarly X-rayed. If the X-ray revealed any suspicious shape such as that of a gun or of an opaque metal box which could conceal a gun or parts of a gun, the procedure would be to request the courier to open the bag for search in the presence of representatives of two embassies, one to be named by the courier and the other by the host country. These representatives would ensure that no documents were examined (though packets of documents could be further X-rayed) but also that the suspicious shapes could be identified and the contents of any containers opaque to X-rays could be removed and themselves X-rayed if necessary. If the couriers declined to open the bag or any suspicious container in it for X-ray he would not be compelled to do so but would be informed that the bag could not be admitted to the country and must be returned to its country of origin. A bag being exported from an embassy would, in similar circumstances, be refused export and returned to the embassy.

If the Economic Summit proposed this system the great majority of countries in the world would probably agree to it. Others, such as Libya, Iraq, and Iran probably would not. The USSR, which is always conscious of the vulnerability of its embassies in maverick countries, might well also agree, after some huffing and puffing. Eventually, the Vienna Convention could be amended but this would take some years so the proposed interim measure should be introduced. Those countries which refused to agree to it could still have their bags subjected to X-ray and excluded if necessary, assuming that they refused the voluntary search.

Another area in which there has been some progress between the more civilized countries is in the judicial field. Proposals for a 'European Judicial Area' have been stillborn because of the enormous difficulty of harmonizing the laws of countries with very different legal traditions, but the best hope will lie in persuading governments that their self-interest lies in voluntary commitments, usually best on a bilateral basis, in enforcing commonly accepted laws.

One of the most encouraging of such agreements is that recently reached and put into practice between the Governments of the Republic of Ireland and the UK, not only to extradite people wanted for terrorist crimes but, where appropriate, to try them in the courts of one country for crimes committed anywhere in the territory of either, with police and other witnesses from either country giving evidence. A number of convictions have been made in this way, as well as extraditions, because it has been clearly recognized by both Governments that the IRA and other illegal paramilitary organizations are their common enemies. This bilateral cooperation has achieved far more than attempts to extend the same kind of agreement on a multinational scale, in which certain countries would always ensure that they left loopholes open to evade the agreement for political reasons when it suited their national interests to do so.

Formal international agreements, even if relatively ineffective in themselves, can, as indicated in the London Summit, provide a basis for cooperation on a working level between police, military, intelligence and administrative officials of civilized countries with mutual goodwill. The Council of Europe in 1977, in conjunction with the Convention mentioned above, set up the TREVI network for this purpose and, at working level without publicity, it has been very effective. So have similar bodies set up within the EEC.

Most effective of all, however, has been the bilateral cooperation (complementary to the above) between officials who can build up a degree of personal trust with each other. These have been particularly effective between West European countries in the police, military and intelligence services.

All of these activities, however, are best carried out by national forces or services in cooperation with rather than by attempting to form joint international anti-terrorist units. There is excellent cooperation between, for example, the anti-terrorist squads of Germany (GSG9), the Netherlands (BBE) and the UK (SAS). When the BBE were handling a train hijack in 1977, for example, they welcomed a liaison team from the GSG9 who, amongst other things, provided frame charges which were ideal for blasting open the doors of the train with minimum risk to the hostages. In the same year the SAS sent a liaison team with stun grenades to assist the GSG9 in rescuing the hostages from an aircraft hijacked to Mogadishu. Many of those involved had already trained together and were on first name terms. This is the best of all kinds of international cooperation.

OPERATIONAL COMMAND AND CONTROL

In a domestic crisis situation, cooperation between the civil, police, military and intelligence services is no less important. The basis of such cooperation must be a top level government crisis management committee embracing whatever departments and services may be involved – the home affairs, defence and foreign ministries and the police, army and intelligence services, etc. In Britain, this committee is known as COBRA. Its stated policies are to maintain the legitimacy of government, control the crisis, deter future incidents and save lives. It coordinates operations on two levels: government strategy and police tactics. The operation of the chain of command can best be illustrated in the context of the seizure and rescue of hostages in the Iranian Embassy in 1980.

On 30 April 1980 six anti-Khomeini gunmen from the Arab province of Khuzestan in Iran seized the Iranian Embassy in Prince's Gate with 26 hostages. These included the British policeman on duty at the door. He pressed his personal alarm signal before he was overpowered and within three minutes the Embassy was surrounded. During five days of patient negotiation it was soon clear that the terrorists did not expect that their demand for the release of 91 prisoners in Iran would be granted and were mainly concerned to get publicity for their cause. Playing on this the negotiators, advised throughout by a psychiatrist, obtained the release of five hostages, most of whom were sick, and ensured that the terrorists were made aware of the times at which BBC broadcasts, including reports of their demands, would be going out. The terrorists were delighted with the publicity they were receiving and the tension eased for a time. They persisted, however, in their demand that they and their Iranian hostages should be given safe conduct out of the country and demanded that three named Arab ambassadors should conduct negotiations at this end. By 5th May they suspected (correctly) that the British Government had no intention of agreeing to this, so they killed a hostage and threatened to kill one more every half hour until the Arab ambassadors arrived. When they pushed the body of the first hostage out into the street, the police officer in command, having no further doubt that they would carry out their threat, asked for authority to send in the SAS rescue team who had been standing by and preparing a rescue plan since the first day. This authority was given by the Home Secretary and the SAS broke in 35 minutes after the body had been pushed out. While they were dealing with the terrorists on the lower floors, other terrorist upstairs shot three more hostages, killing one of them, before the SAS could reach them. The SAS killed five of the terrorists. The sixth initially masqueraded as a hostage but was later spotted and arrested. No one else on either side was hurt.

The policy was controlled thoughout by COBRA. The police officer in charge on the scene interpreted COBRA's policy in the negotiations and controlled the tactics throughout. The SAS were responsible to him, not to the Ministry of Defence. He took the initiative and obtained COBRA approval to send them in, giving them the task of rescuing the hostages. How they carried out this task was a matter for the SAS officer, and his soldiers carried it out under his orders without interference from the police. This took them less than 20 minutes, and then they handed the surviving terrorist, the hostages and the building back to the police.

A very important aspect of this kind of operation is liaison with the media. Generally (apart from the controversial smuggling of a television camera into a window overlooking the back of the Embassy where the SAS assault went in) this cooperation was excellent. One reason for this was that six months earlier, by chance, the BBC had conducted a study and training exercise in conjunction with the police, other journalists, politicians, civil servants etc, based on a scenario uncannily similar to the actual siege. The exercise took the form of a 'hypothetical' (a technique developed by the Harvard Law School) in which some 20 people played roles similar to those which they might play in their working lives. The part of the police officer in charge was played by the police officer who was in the event to be in charge at Prince's Gate, John Dellow. The Editor of BBC television news (Alan Protheroe) and the television reporter who reported the actual rescue on the scene six months later (Kate Adie) were both playing the roles they were soon to play in practice. So were the Editor of the *Daily Mirror* and one of his reporters. The results proved the value – and the importance – of this kind of study and training.

Ironically, the Ayatollah Khomeini was holding all the US Embassy staff as hostages in Tehran at this time while the British were rescuing his Embassy staff from Iranian Arab dissidents in London. Communication with the Iranian Government was, in the circumstances, surprisingly good and they fully approved of Mrs Thatcher's firm line and her refusal to give the terrorists safe conduct.

Had the Embassy and hostages been from a friendly country, such as Germany or the USA, there would undoubtedly have been a close liaison with their representatives in London or with a minister or official sent over specially. As indicated in the previous section, however, the actual operation would still have been conducted by national security forces under a national crisis management committee. Neither the training and morale of the police and SAS rescue squad, nor the speed and sureness of COBRA's policy decisions, would have been the same if they had been other than single nation bodies acting in their own country.

GOVERNMENT POLICY ON NEGOTIATION WITH TERRORISTS

When terrorists are applying their coercion directly on a government, most governments have now learned that it is necessary to stand firm, as Mrs Thatcher's did at Prince's Gate. The US Government has also made it clear that, when their diplomats overseas are hostages, they will neither make concessions themselves nor ask the host government to do so to save the hostages' lives. US (and British) diplomats accept this hazard in the same way that soldiers do. While some concessions may be made over peripheral matters such as publicity, they recognize that it is folly to permit proven terrorists to go free, not only because it will encourage others but also because experience has shown that the freed terrorists will almost always use their freedom (and the prestige they have gained thereby) to organize more terrorist actions and will usually kill more people with their own hands. After five convicted terrorists were released by the West Berlin Government in exchange for the life of Peter Lorenz in 1975, one of these five is known to have shot two more people dead at the OPEC kidnapping in Vienna a few months later.

It is, however, unrealistic for a government to work on the

assumption that either families or corporations will act in this way when one of their family or firm is held hostage. Some governments (like in Italy and Argentina) have attempted to impose laws to prevent the payment of ransoms to criminals or terrorists but these have almost invariably been counter-productive. No matter how much he may agree with them in principle, a father will override any such law which he sees to be preventing him from saving the life of his child. Similarly, a corporation will not allow the law to force it to abandon one of its executives to his fate because, apart from ethical reasons, it knows that the price it would pay for doing so, in terms of staff morale, would be greater. Soldiers and diplomats accept that they may have to die for their country but businessmen do not accept any obligation to die for their company and parents and spouses will not sacrifice the lives of their families even if they would sacrifice their own.

The effect of such laws in practice is to induce both corporations and families to negotiate and settle with criminals or terrorists behind the backs of the police, as happened repeatedly in Italy and Argentina in the 1970s. This means that they will pay a bigger ransom more quickly, and that, worse still, they will deny the police any possibility of obtaining intelligence or evidence for conviction, for which the only source is the contact maintained by negotiation. The best course for the police is to offer every assistance to the negotiators, to persuade them that the best hope of saving the life of the hostage is to keep negotiations in progress, and to encourage them to keep the police fully informed over these negotiations so that they can rescue the victim and arrest the kidnappers.

The FBI in the USA have shown the way in this respect. They convince the family or firm from the start that their first priority is the safe release of the victim and that the arrest of the kidnappers is secondary. The result of this, paradoxically, is greatly to increase the chances of arrest and conviction. A Rand Corporation study in 1974 reported that, of 647 cases of kidnapping over a 40-year period (1934–74) all but three had been solved and over 90 per cent of the kidnappers had been captured. There can have been few crimes of any kind with such a high detection rate and this testifies to the wisdom of the FBI's approach.

Governments can best help themselves, the police, the kidnap victims and the community if they pass laws which help negotiation and apprehension of kidnappers and refrain from passing laws which inhibit them.

Laws which help include, above all, those which control the possession and movement of weapons, ammunition and explosives; also laws which inhibit the movements of criminals and terrorists, internally and across frontiers; laws which assist intelligence, detection, arrest and the gathering of evidence for conviction; laws which facilitate the custody of suspects to give time for investigation without prejudicing the civil liberties of innocent people; and laws which enable liberal forms of justice to operate effectively by preventing the intimidation of witnesses, juries and judges, the deliberate delay or disruption of Court proceedings and the abuse of the privileges accorded to lawyers in a free society.

Laws which hinder negotiation and thereby reduce the chance of detection, arrest and conviction of the kidnappers include, as described above, the banning of payment of ransoms and, in some countries, making it a criminal offence to communicate with criminal and terrorist gangs. Judges in Italy have sometimes ordered the freezing of the assets of a corporation or a family negotiating for the release of a victim, or restricting the release of currency; this, however, has merely led large numbers of rich parents or companies to break currency regulations by building up large bank balances or other assets outside the country. Also, in some European and Latin American countries, attempts have been made to ban insurance against extortion, but here again the families and firms under threat have simply placed their insurance outside the country. This ban is also counter-productive in two other ways: first, because the insurance underwriters (like fire insurance companies) take positive steps to improve their client's security against kidnap and any other potential grounds for extortion; and secondly because, if the client is subjected to extortion, they provide professional advice on conducting negotiations. Since the client has probably never been subjected to extortion before and the advisers sent by the underwriters have conducted many, the negotiations are much more likely to be successful and to acquire useful information and evidence for the police. For all these reasons, the chances of a kidnap taking place and the size of any ransom paid out are both on average much lower for insured than for uninsured people. This should not cause any surprise because no one would suggest that taking out fire insurance increases the risk of fire.

The conclusion is that the governments and police should do all in their power to help and nothing to inhibit people negotiating in the face of extortion. The success of this policy is convincingly proved by the figures quoted above for the FBI.

SUMMARY OF TRENDS FOR THE FUTURE

The probable trends in crime and political violence were discussed in earlier chapters: greater affluence will lead to more rather than less crime; disappointed idealism, frustration and boredom amongst young people, especially the more educated ones, will give rise to more demonstrations sometimes exploding into violence; greater interdependence and centralization will make new key points more attractive as terrorist targets, especially in the fields of data processing, communications, energy and transport; public familiarity will encourage bigger and more spectacular bombs to attract the attention of the media; guns will become smaller and more lethal with more sophisticated sights; better bank security and reduced circulation of cash will encourage more extortion by kidnap and threat of violence or disruption; and all of these things will add to the power of people who have entered restricted premises by stealth or deception to do damage or to extort money and concessions.

Recent years have seen an alarming increase in the abuse of diplomatic privileges accorded under the Vienna Convention. The assumption of the right to sweep aside respect for human life, international agreements or moral principles in the name of God gives cause for concern. The religious fanaticism which breeds this attitude, especially Islamic fundamentalism, shows every sign of increasing and the positive desire for martyrdom which this can engender makes it particularly dangerous.

For all these reasons, governments will need to pay increasing attention to intelligence and to controlling access to their own vulnerable premises; also to assist corporations and other citizens to do the same. The technological means for improving these things already exist and are likely to develop further with the microelectronics revolution. The constraints on their use are likely to be political and social rather than technical. It will be desirable for governments to have contingency plans to introduce some of the measures available – such as identity cards and passports with electronically recorded data to prevent forgery or impersonation, and the recording of more personal data – in case a sudden upsurge of violence makes these things necessary to save lives. The contingency plans must, however, also contain effective safeguards to control the power which these aids will place in the hands of officials lest it be abused to the prejudice of civil liberties. Such abuse would alienate public support and would also be likely in the long term to undermine the foundations and stability of democratic societies.

The very rapid development of dissemination of information direct into every home, both from outside agencies by satellite and through domestic multichannel communications media, will give constantly growing power both to governments and to those who wish to destabilize the society; this power could be exercised to manipulate public opinion, raise or undermine confidence and induce prejudice, hatred, fear or hysteria. To guard against such abuse, either by officials, by commercial organizations, by political movements or by foreign governments, will require great vigilance, and full use will need to be made of the developing technology available to exercise this vigilance. Continuous government research will be needed to assess the likely effects of developing technology and developing attitudes, and to study the best means of using the technology to give the community greater security, greater freedom and more options in their lives rather than less.

Governments will also need to give guidance and support to corporations and citizens in improving their own security and freedom from manipulation or coercion.

The speed with which domestic or international crises can develop will necessitate improvement in national crisis management organizations and international (especially bilateral) liaison between government departments, intelligence, police and anti-terrorist forces.

Government crisis management committees should also have a contingency planning role. As protection of one kind of target or against one kind of terrorist attack improves, the terrorists will seek others. (The growth of extortion as robbery becomes more difficult is one example already quoted.) It will be necessary for contingency planners to foresee the coming changes and their likely consequences so that they can prepare for them and alert the community to do so too.

8 Corporate Response and Guidelines for Security

RISK MANAGEMENT

A corporation facing the risk of malicious violence in the years ahead can be compared with a farmer facing the risk of natural disasters: fires, floods, droughts or gales. He cannot forecast the weather for a year or even a month ahead but he knows that he is likely to have to face most of these hazards at some time in his working life in varying degrees of severity. He does not know which will hit him, or how, or when, but he studies the form that each is likely to take from past experience tempered by his prediction of changing circumstances. He then takes precautionary measures to minimize the damage that any of them can do him and he diversifies to ensure that none of them can ruin him completely. Thereafter he keeps his precautions in good shape.

No risk can be removed entirely, but some can be reduced to a negligible level. There are also certain risks which a corporation must accept, either because they are so remote that they can be ignored, or because the cost of preventing them is too high in relation to the potential cost of damage, or because the corporation must rely on the government to cover them (from attack by terrorists firing missiles from long range, for example). The corporation can, however, reduce the likelihood of it being picked as a target, or reduce the scale of damage if it is attacked, by good routine security.

Wise contingency planning will identify some risks which, though currently remote, could suddenly become serious – for instance, if an unexpected collapse of order were to make expatriate residences or travel between home and work too vulnerable to accept. Examples of this was the sudden deterioration of the situation in Iran in 1978–79 and in El Salvador in 1979–80. Contingency plans for such emergencies should allow for such things as relocation, movement in escorted convoys, evacuation of families or, in the last resort, total evacuation of personnel and movable assets of a threatened subsidiary.

Some risks can be transferred in part – at least the financial part – by insurance. This will be done as a matter of course for fire, theft, floods etc, but may well be extended to cover terrorist attack, kidnap and extortion.

Most risks, however, fall into a middle category. They cannot be wholly prevented but they are potentially too damaging to be ignored, so they must be reduced and plans made to minimize their effect if they do materialize. The approach to these risks is exactly the same as to the risk of fire. The fire officer assesses the risk to various parts of his premises and the cost of the damage it could do. He arranges to transfer most of the direct financial risk by insurance, but a fire would still be highly disruptive, so he considers the various measures available for reducing the risk and the various measures available for fighting it if it occurs. He estimates the cost of each of these measures, not only in money but also in terms of loss of efficiency, loss of profitability, harassment, trade union relations and staff morale. Taking all these costs into account he decides (or puts a proposal to his Board to approve) how much he can spend on reducing the risk and on preparing to fight it, makes a plan and puts it into effect.

As with the risk of fire, so with the risks of crime, mob violence and terrorism. The remainder of this chapter re-examines these risks in the light of the methods available, or likely to become available, for reducing or fighting them, and suggests guidelines for security planning. These are presented primarily in the context of risk management by a corporation against the threats to property and personnel, with qualifications where appropriate for family or government targets.

DEVELOPMENT OF SECURITY EQUIPMENT

The microelectronics revolution will offer continuing scope for improvement of security equipment. The big security firms competing for the market will focus their research on areas most in demand and on areas in which the most significant breakthroughs might occur. In some areas there will be problems in controlling the use of these developments to avoid prejudicing civil liberties; these areas include personnel selection, proof of identity, access control and some aspects of surveillance. Other areas are less controversial such as perimeter security (though this does involve surveillance); alarm systems; blocking of access against demonstrators, rioters, gunmen and bombers; detection of weapons and explosives; security of the product against interference or pollution; security of storage of commercial data, and of communications (cable, fibre-optic and microwave – or of new methods which emerge); security against eavesdropping (bugging and sweeping); and security against personal attack and kidnap, including travel security. These will be discussed in their context later in the chapter.

PERSONNEL SELECTION AND VETTING

'The strongest castle walls are not proof against a traitor within'. For modern industry and commerce, devastating disruption or espionage can be achieved by one malicious person gaining access to one key point. The most vital security will lie in detecting and excluding unreliable people in the personnel selection stage; in detecting signs of a staff member becoming alienated or coming under pressure (possibly involving his family) to betray confidence, with particular attention to those with access to key points such as computer rooms, software stores or confidential papers; and in good access control with effective checks on identity and impersonation – again especially for access to key points.

There is justifiable public anxiety about the possible infringement of civil liberties which would arise from full use even of the technology that is already available for this kind of security. The potential power of governments and managements inherent in the recording and storage of personal data could be – and without stringent safeguards undoubtedly would be – abused. Especially at risk in this context are a person's credit-worthiness or suitability for employment. The problem was discussed in a police and intelligence context in Chapter 6. For commercial firms, the issue is less clear cut. It is usually accepted that, *if asked*, a company should give a frank appraisal of a former employee to another company. On the other hand, some people will argue that this should only be done with the knowledge and consent of the person concerned – if he or she has named the company as a reference. But even if giving such information in writing were subject to restriction it would be virtually impossible to prevent a manager in one firm giving an oral opinion in conversation with his opposite number in another. Such information can, perhaps unwittingly, be false, exaggerated, unproven and, of course, highly damaging to the victim. As in the police and intelligence context, this must ultimately depend on integrity, supplemented by the laws of defamation, but there is no real answer to it until and unless some future development produces a really reliable means of detecting a lie.

Yet, before a firm employs someone in a sensitive area as described, it is essential that it has some means of establishing whether he or she can be trusted. At present this depends on the astuteness and judgement of those conducting the selection interviews and thereafter on a vigilant, perceptive and highly personal degree of management. As technological development puts more power into the hands of the state and of senior executives, the means of monitoring the use of it must be developed in parallel; and to ensure the integrity of those who hold such power, selection and continued vetting of top management is the most important safeguard of all.

ACCESS CONTROL, IDENTIFICATION AND IMPERSONATION

Vigilance in selecting and vetting sensitive staff must be accompanied by strict access control and the control of visitors, including workers employed by contractors for construction, installation, repair and maintenance. This control will depend upon a sound system of permanent and temporary identity cards, with quick and reliable means of detecting forgery and impersonation. While the introduction of national identity cards is controversial (see Chapter 6), few will question the need for staff who have access to sensitive areas in either government or commercial premises to carry reliable proof of identity.

As criminals and political terrorists become more sophisticated, the case for more stringent means of identification will be justified. Forged identity cards can now be detected quite easily provided that they carry electronically recorded magnetic data and the necessary equipment to read that data is installed and used conscientiously. There is, however, a need for better methods of guarding against impersonation, for instance, to ensure that someone presenting a genuine card is not impersonating the holder (assuming that the holder has been prevented from notifying its theft or loss). These methods must be simple and quick enough to avoid imposing delay on staff checking in at the start of the day.

The most promising means of detecting impersonation is to match magnetic data on the card to a palm print, the palm being placed on the machine simultaneously with the card being inserted. A voice print match could be equally quick. In case either of these registered doubt (sometimes, perhaps, due to a malfunction) more deliberate checks could be made by matching other idiosyncratic features such as the dynamic characteristics of a signature, done to order, or the analysis of saliva, either of which is as unique as a palm or finger print. These confirmatory checks could be done within a minute or less, on a separate machine, without interrupting the normal flow of people checking in. A possible further confirmatory check would be to record a sufficient number of other personal features – height, colour of eyes, scars etc, in the magnetic data on the card to make it impracticable for any imposter to match them all.

There would be resistance to this from trade unions and civil liberties lobbies because it would be seen as the thin end of the wedge, enabling the state or corporation to extend the system to spy on citizens in other ways. This resistance would provide a healthy restraint on abuse. A necessary safeguard would lie in ensuring that the preparation and use of these cards and of the data on them are exclusive to the company; also that the holder knows, and can check with some kind of ombudsman organization, precisely what is recorded on his card. This would not prejudice security because the knowledge that the palm print or voice print is recorded will not enable anyone to forge it.

It will be important to select the best psychological moment to introduce such a system, like in the wake of some violent crime or terrorist incident involving penetration of the security screen and possibly also injury or loss of life. Notice can also reasonably be given at any time that appointments giving access to sensitive information or facilities will, from a certain date, be conditional on voluntary acceptance of this security system.

VIOLENT CRIME

All the indications are that violent crime will increase in both rich and poor countries, and that in rich countries it will go on getting more sophisticated. As robbery becomes more difficult, extortion is likely to increase especially in three fields: by kidnap or threat to kidnap; by threat of product pollution; and by threat to disrupt key facilities (such as computer centres) by interference with software or by sabotage and bombing. In all cases the art of extortion will lie in pitching the size of the demand for a quick settlement at a level which is substantially lower than the likely cost of resisting it.

The first line of defence will be to use the available developments in technology to improve perimeter security, surveillance, alarms, access control and identification; also to improve cooperation with police in crime prevention and intelligence. All of these measures will pay dividends in security against other kinds of threat.

RIOTS, DEMONSTRATIONS, DISRUPTION AND SABOTAGE

The widening gap between rich and poor countries and within the poorer societies themselves, coupled with their growing population and urbanization, will cause rising frustration in the shanty towns around large African, Asian and Latin American cities. This will lead not only to a growth in violent crime in these cities but possibly also to rioting. There is an inevitable risk of both of these affecting foreign embassies, foreign firms and expatriate residents, especially as there is now a widespread resentment against the part played by Western countries – for

example by demanding higher interest on outstanding debts – in
causing their poverty. This is almost certain to get worse, and
should be borne in mind in contingency planning in almost all
Third World countries.

In the industrialized countries the new society that will
develop during the microelectronics revolution will provide
more leisure and greater affluence for the majority, with a
higher minimum standard of living for those on social security
but with wider income differentials between those who reap the
benefits and those who do not – especially those who have been
educated but prefer to drop out of the rat race. These have
historically provided the main stream of dissent in almost every
society. Their dissent will take the form of trying to block and
disrupt the smooth running and prosperity of the society they
reject. The growing interdependence of this society, in
administrative, industrial and commercial fields, will provide
more and more attractive targets as key points for this
disruption.

New philosophies for dissent and disruption will emerge as
they always have: the relatively less violent demonstrators and
dropouts of the 1960s gave way to the much more lethal
Trotskyist revolutionaries of the 1970s; then the fanatical
Islamic fundamentalists and the 'undogmatic' or 'diffuse'
guerrillas emerged as leaders of fashion in the 1980s. The latter
philosophy – that of the Revolutionary Cells in Germany – may
prove to be the fastest growing fashion, especially in Europe,
because the cells are hard to detect, attack property rather than
lives and are particularly disruptive to the modern
interdependent industrial and commercial society. They will be
a major threat to industries connected with defence, energy
and electronics; also to government and commercial
organizations whose computerized storage and communications
are vulnerable to disruption.

The information explosion and growing public familiarity
with blood on the screen will encourage more sensational
violence to attract media attention, probably with greater
collaboration between the 'diffuse' guerrillas and protest
demonstrations in Europe.

Corporations and families will have to rely primarily on good
government intelligence and policing to prevent demonstrators
and rioters from overwhelming their installations. They can,

however, make themselves less attractive as targets by good security. In particular they should ensure that they have strong and secure perimeters; also robust access barriers, both outside and between the entrance lobby and the interior of the building. The latter should have alternative means of closure, either by entrance lobby staff or by a security guard from a secure observation post within the building to avoid the risk of being rushed. It is important not to forget side and rear entrances and the access points to utilities (for ventilation, delivery of fuel, maintenance etc.) which are often less well protected and guarded. Alarm systems and direct communications to the police (duplicated if possible by radio) are also desirable.

Governments and corporations (whether operating in their own countries or as overseas subsidiaries) should have contingency plans not only for terrorism but also for the worst cases of escalation of rioting and disorder. Depending upon the country, these could include mass peaceful demonstrations (like those one million strong in Tehran in 1978) which get out of hand or which panic when fired on by trigger-happy soldiers or police; or clashes between rival factions (left, right or religious); or large-scale violence amounting to civil war.

BOMBS AND HOAX BOMB CALLS

The huge truck bombs placed by Shia terrorists in Lebanon and Kuwait in 1983 led to the withdrawal of the multinational force from Lebanon, the withdrawal of the US naval, air and land forces being seen as a particular triumph. This kind of attack is likely to increase as a result of that success; also because the kind of concern for public opinion which exercises some restraint on left-wing terrorists has little effect on those inspired by right-wing, racialist or religious philosophies. The sacrifice of suicide drivers is a feature of religious fanaticism but determined volunteers are still likely to be rare, so greater use of remote control must be expected, not only for firing (as already done), but also possibly for guiding the vehicle on its final approach.

The most important defence will be to keep any unauthorized vehicle from getting within the building, like a loading bay, courtyard or underground car park, whether driven in forcibly or by stealth. This will necessitate robust barriers with efficient identification and control. Ideally they should be robust enough to withstand attempts to crash through them, and should be adequately covered by police or security guards, carrying arms in countries where that is the norm.

Next in importance will be to block off any adjacent areas in which vehicles might park which have direct access to a public highway, as well as having controlled barriers for normal entry into official vehicle parks within the compound from which vehicles might gain access to the outside or inside of the building.

If the threat justifies it, half width concrete obstacles (or heavy bollards which can be anchored or removed) should be positioned so as to compel approaching vehicles to slow down and execute a fairly tight zig-zag. This will not only reduce the likelihood of the barrier itself being rushed; it will also make it extremely difficult for a remotely controlled vehicle to negotiate it.

A further precaution, which ideally should have been incorporated in the design of the building, is to avoid siting any facility which is crucial to the functioning of the building (for example a computer centre, main switchboard, telephone exchange or pumping station) adjacent to an outside wall even within the complex; especially not a wall close to a public highway or to a possible parking space for vehicles.

Parcel and letter bombs can at present be reliably detected by X-ray or by explosive sniffers or both. The statutory tagging and strict control of manufactured detonators and explosives (see Chapter 6) would greatly enhance the prospects of detection of all kinds of bombs, not just those sent by mail, but its effect will be limited unless there is general international enforcement of the system and this, sadly, is unlikely.

The control of bombs brought in by hand, in brief cases, shopping bags, packets or cartons of supplies should be part of routine access control and search, with all staff trained to be vigilant, not just those at the gate.

For the reasons given in Chapter 5, nuclear, chemical and biological weapons have not been and are not likely to be used, but there may be hoax calls or threats that they will be used, as there have been in the past.

Hoax calls, also discussed in Chapter 5, can cause as much disruption as real bomb calls. Political terrorist organizations want their threats to be credible and may wish to avoid the adverse public reaction to massive casualties, so they sometimes arrange a code to satisfy the police that their call is genuine. On occasions the hoax caller is clearly unconvincing or may be tripped up by questions from the telephone operator but when in doubt hoax calls must initially be treated as real. To reduce the risk of being traced, telephoned bomb warnings are likely to be very short, and communicated to the first person to answer – usually an operator or secretary. All of these, therefore, should be trained and provided with proformas showing questions to be asked and details to be noted (the accent of the caller, for example). Then, to minimize disruption, all staff should be trained to search their own areas of work simultaneously; they are the people most likely to spot anything unusual, but they should have on call a specially trained bomb search team whose task would be to block off and if possible muffle any suspicious object, decide what areas need to be evacuated and call the police bomb disposal squad. (Bomb search must not be confused with bomb disposal.)

Tracing short telephone calls will always be difficult especially if they come by direct dialling from a foreign country. It would, in fact, be *technically* feasible for telephone authorities, even international ones, to pinpoint the instrument of origin of any such call within a few seconds on the pressing of a panic button by the person receiving the call; the technology would be much the same as that for routing the calls and recording the charges. This, however, is most unlikely to be politically feasible due to difficulties in finance, international cooperation and coordination, and considerations of civil liberties.

DATA STORAGE AND COMMUNICATIONS

Catastrophic damage and expense can be caused by sabotage of computer hardware and software or electronic interference with computer systems and communications, and the importance of selection of staff and control of access, were discussed earlier in this chapter. In case these fail, however, and a malicious person does gain access to the hardware or software, there should be as much duplication of data as possible.

Industrial espionage is a growth area. There is continuous

development of equipment for bugging and counter-bugging, and for eavesdropping on data communication. Cable communications are the easiest to tap. Microwave transmissions of digital data are being made faster and more secure by such devices as packet switching systems, frequency hopping, burst transmission and modern cryptology but there is a continual battle between these and the development of means of intercepting and decoding them. Fibre optics currently provide the most secure means of communication and, as in any young science, there is every prospect of rapid development but there is also a persistent search for means of tapping into them. The development of intelligent terminals (for instance with extensive memories of their own) means that there may in the future be a reduction in the need to communicate sensitive data either by cable, fibre optics or microwave.

It is expensive both to secure and to tap communications and one sinister effect of this may be to tempt extreme political movements and small terrorist groups to become more dependent on the USSR who, through the KGB, already devote huge funds to eavesdropping almost every major international channel for financial, commercial and governmental transactions.

LONG-RANGE WEAPONS

Protection against long-range missiles fired at buildings or vehicles must primarily depend on the general level of security achieved by government, police, military and intelligence services. Siting of buildings or installations can greatly affect their attractiveness as targets and it may even be possible and desirable to buy blocks of flats overlooking these buildings for use as staff accommodation or for renting to selected tenants; or to build new ones to shield vulnerable facilities from long-range fire. Such facilities are, again, less vulnerable if sited away from outside walls.

PRODUCT EXTORTION

The growing menace of extortion or malicious discredit by threat of product pollution was discussed in Chapter 5. Thus far, this crime seems to have had a relatively poor record of success but a partial explanation for this impression may be that, if a corporation does pay a ransom, it will certainly try to keep the story out of the media and may not even report it to the police. Another reason may be that a large proportion of the attempts so far have been by small-time criminals or cranks rather than by sophisticated criminal gangs or political groups.

A corporation faced with this type of threat has in practice a good chance of handling it successfully if it has prepared itself physically and psychologically to do so. This is best achieved by having a standing Crisis Management Committee (CMC) and this is discussed more fully, in relation to all types of crisis and extortion, at the end of the chapter. An effective CMC will have foreseen the possible forms of the threat and will have taken certain policy decisions in advance. It will also, in view of the gravity of the issues involved, have geared itself to set up an immediate negotiating team with a full-time coordinator to handle the crisis.

The CMC's first task will be to establish the credibility of the threat (by analysing the poisoned samples, for example, which will usually be indicated in the threat) and judge whether it comes from a crank, an amateur or a sophisticated criminal or terrorist. It should already have decided its policy regarding the police (probably to inform a named and trusted police officer with whom the hazards of such a crisis have been discussed); also its policy on dealing with the media.

It will need to reconcile three sometimes conflicting considerations: commercial, moral and public policy. Even a rumour can cause a huge loss of trade; for example, when a recent product pollution threat against a large UK supermarket chain was leaked to the media, the losses in sales were estimated at £1 000 000. The extortioners themselves, however, are unlikely to leak the story except as a last resort because once it is out most of the damage is done so the company has little incentive to pay a ransom. A meticulous search coupled with an immediate withdrawal of stock will incur heavy staff overtime but is probably worth it, because whatever the company does must subsequently be publicly and legally defensible or the long-term losses may be even greater. They would be greater still if any customer or staff member died or became seriously ill. (There has been no reported case of this except in the Tylenol incident – see Chapter 5 – which was probably not an extortion case but a malicious intention to kill in order to damage the company.)

Since, in almost every case, the aim of the criminals is to obtain money, they are unlikely to burn their boats at once, and will probably be ready to negotiate, though they will threaten otherwise. The experience of known cases indicates that, if there is discreet police cooperation, and if the media do not report the case (due either to successful secrecy or to a voluntary blackout) there will be a very good chance that the criminals will be arrested before payment of a ransom or at least so soon afterwards that the ransom is recovered. As with other risks, insurance will reduce the pressure on the company, widen its freedom of action in negotiation and, of course, limit its financial loss, so this too is likely to improve the likelihood of a successful conclusion.

PERSONAL ATTACK, INTIMIDATION, KIDNAPPING AND HOSTAGE TAKING

Personal attack, kidnap and intimidation in order to extort money or to drive governments or corporations to cease operations in a country are likely to increase as indicated in Chapter 5. The threat may be directed at expatriate or local staff or both. Staff and families are most vulnerable on the road between home and work (or school). Most at risk are senior officials and executives and their best defence is normally to keep a low profile, varying their routes and their times, and travelling unobtrusively in unostentatious vehicles; in other words to be unpredictable and, as far as possible, unrecognizable.

If a low profile is impracticable because of the prominence and uniqueness of the target (like a Head of State), the only alternative will be a quantum leap to sufficient protection to overcome the anticipated maximum level of threat. If the threat is from a strong and sophisticated political organization the scale of protection may be very large – as in the case of VIPs such as the President of the United States, or King Hussein of Jordan. Inadequate protection (for instance, Aldo Moro's four bodyguards) may do more harm than good, by attracting attention to the target without being able to prevent it from being overwhelmed.

If a threat reaches too high a level (large-scale terrorism, lawlessness or civil war) a government or corporation may have to choose between withdrawing its operation or rehousing its staff in defended compounds, moving only in escorted convoys (or by helicopter) to secure places of work. This is not so difficult as it may seem, and has been done on a number of occasions. It is, however, frustrating for staff and very expensive if it goes on for a long time, so it will only be seriously contemplated if the continuance of the operation is considered essential for political or commercial reasons. Nevertheless, it is a wise precaution to have contingency plans for such relocation and protection ready in case of emergency in order to retain a range of options other than forced and precipitate evacuation.

There has been an ugly increase in recent years, especially in Italy, in the kidnapping of children to extort money from rich parents. It may be wise for families likely to be subject to extortion to harden the normal anti-theft protection of their residences by adding more sophisticated surveillance and alarm systems up to factory or bank standards, including alternative communications (preferably by radio) to the police. As with executives themselves, however, the most important time for protection will be when the children are on the road – going to or from school, for example, or to or from such things as evening classes or leisure activities. Wherever possible, the children should both get into and get out of the car within a secure perimeter, at home and at the school. Since there may be little scope for varying routes and times to school, groups of children should travel in convoy when this is justified by the threat; and schools should be warned never in any circumstances allow them to be collected by anyone other than a positively authorized and recognizable person.

In some countries, especially in Latin America, there have been cases of older school children or university students being befriended by fellow students who are in fact being employed by terrorist groups (or, in the case of universities, being members of them) to act as spies for information on family movements or, in some cases, to secure invitations to the home with a view to collaboration in an attack on the family. In one case the daughter's 'friend' was invited for the night and personally placed a bomb under the father's bed which killed him the next night. Parents should warn their children and be vigilant.

One further precaution is to discipline the children not to unlock the door to anyone other than specific people about whose identity there is no risk of doubt.

The response to a kidnap and to a demand for a ransom will have a better chance of success if it has been foreseen by a Crisis Management Committee which has contingency plans for dealing with it. This will be discussed later in this chapter. The essential element in response to a kidnap is to play for time, since it is most unlikely that kidnappers will destroy their bargaining potential by killing their victims at once. Negotiation in discreet cooperation with the police will increase the chances of locating the hideout and of detection, arrest and conviction of the kidnappers.

Hostage seizures in known locations (in embassies or corporate premises) have little appeal for criminals and are likely to indicate a political terrorist group, probably aiming primarily for publicity. Again, they will be reluctant to kill their hostages, so patient negotiation has a good chance of success, backed by a highly trained rescue force, preferably one with a reputation which will encourage the hostage-takers to give in before it is launched. Better still, a rescue force with a high reputation may discourage such attempts from being made at all.

Hijacking has been greatly reduced since 1973 by effective searching of passengers and baggage for guns or explosives before they enter the aircraft. As a result, hijackers are increasingly using forms of threat other than metallic guns and bombs – plastic replica guns and inflammable or noxious fluids. If he judges that the lives of passengers are at risk, the captain of an aircraft has little option but to land as directed, though he may be able to use technical arguments (fuel or landing criteria) to divert to an airport in a country in which the subsequent negotiations or rescue are likely to be successfully handled. Once the aircraft is on the ground, negotiation becomes similar to that in any other siege, but will depend a great deal on international cooperation as discussed in Chapter 7.

CONTINGENCY PLANNING AND CRISIS MANAGEMENT

The growing threat of criminal and political violence, and especially of bombing and extortion, makes it imperative that every government and corporate organization in a high risk country establishes a Crisis Management Committee (CMC), some of whose purposes have been discussed earlier in their various contexts. Governments themselves will need CMCs at the centre (like that discussed in Chapter 7) and a Crisis Management Team (CMT) or Local Negotiating Team (LNT) at each of its embassies etc. Similarly, there should be a CMC at the corporate headquarters of any multinational which has operations in high risk areas, with CMTs or LNTs trained to respond to crises in its subsidiaries.

The first function of these committees and teams will be to assess the various threats and to review and improve security against them. Next they will prepare contingency plans for action in the event of this security failing to prevent a crisis. These plans will attempt to foresee as many as possible of the difficult decisions which are likely to arise and to establish a policy in advance (for example, about the immediate response to bomb threats, cooperation with the police, dealing with the media, negotiation, payment of ransoms and safeguarding other potential targets which might be threatened in order to increase the pressure). The CMC should establish and train CMTs and LNTs as necessary, and organize seminars and simulation exercises so that they are ready for the problems which will arise and, equally important, so that they can adjust their plans to meet the constant changes which will occur in the environment, the political climate and the fashions of terrorism and crime.

In the case of a corporation and its subsidiaries, one of the primary tasks of CMCs and CMTs will be to establish a means whereby commercial operations can continue with minimum disruption during a crisis which, especially in the case of a kidnap, may last for several weeks or months. The essence of this will be to select in advance a suitable executive to be relieved of other duties and devote his full time to handling the crisis. This will save a great deal more than his salary. He may be able to handle it from day to day with only one or two advisers, coopting others as needed when particular decisions arise (financial, legal, public relations, trade union or personnel management).

The most important dividend of all such preparations, and especially of the work of the CMC, will be to create a level of security which is manifestly higher than that in other similar targets – so high that would-be criminals and terrorists are deterred and that crises do not therefore materialize at all. The most enduring lesson of the past, which will apply equally to the future, is that the corporation or family or individual with the best security is seldom picked as a target. Criminals and terrorists, if they are to succeed in an operation against a sophisticated and well-protected target, will conduct a thorough surveillance in order to find weak links and make a plan. If that surveillance reveals a positive attitude towards security, and a greater awareness than that of others, they will almost always turn away to seek an easier target.

Part II

Regional Assessments

9 Europe

PETER JANKE

Non-criminal violence stems from a number of sources in Europe, the most fecund being terrorism motivated by ethnic sensitivities. As virulent, but more transitory in nature, is the so-called armed struggle promoted by ideologically disaffected groups. From abroad, the continent is at risk from terrorist incidents arising from the Arab–Israeli dispute, from the Islamic fundamentalist revolution and from Armenian attacks on Turkish targets. At a lower level of direct action, issue groups are intent upon imposing change by breaking the law. Communal violence of a spontaneous nature, though it may lead to arson, is of no interest in discussion of premeditated political violence which is causing or could cause acts of terrorism.

ETHNIC TERRORISM

Today, areas of Europe worst affected by political violence are Northern Ireland, the Spanish Basque Country and Corsica. In these cases the conflict is rooted in long-standing disputes with central government based upon demands made by separatist nationalists who threaten the historic unity of nation states.

Those who wage these campaigns are organised in groups that in the first instance practise terrorism against the state, but which also attack commercial enterprise. The Provisional Irish Republican Army (PIRA), Freedom for the Basque Homeland (ETA) and the Corsican National Front (FNLC) do not have the remotest chance of wringing from central government the kind of governmental concessions likely to cause them to desist from terrorist acts. On the other hand, despite the intellectual and financial resources available, confident democratic governments have not been able to bring about a solution. At best the level of insecurity has been contained.

Geographical containment is harder. There is every reason for the Irish bomber to seek out his target on the British mainland. In this respect the assassination attempt against Mrs Thatcher and her cabinet colleagues at the Conservative Party Conference in Brighton on 12 October 1984 was but another spectacular incident, in the long endeavour to wrest control of Ulster from the Protestant majority in the province. Irish terrorism can from time to time reach out to the European mainland, but targets will be largely confined to British diplomatic and consular facilities.

Mainland France will experience increasing terrorism from the Basque and Corsican problems. The Spanish Basque problem spills over the Pyrenees touching the sensitivities of French Basques. To date this overlap has been minimal, largely confined to isolated bombings in protest against the tourist trade, and to sudden death which Spanish rightists, or gunmen hired for the purpose, have dealt to Spanish Basques using the French Basque Country as a refuge from Spanish justice. The dangers were indicated in October 1984, when President Mitterrand made only the second visit to the region by a French president this century so as to explain his decision to extradite three Spanish Basques to face trial in Spain.

Because the Corsican separatists have failed to bring about a French withdrawal from the island they have sought to strengthen their impact by bombing mainland targets. As trials are held, so protest explosions will grow in number and size and French banks as well as judicial and state targets will be bombed.

The second half of the 1980s will see the persistence of terrorism from these three ethnic sources, with consequences not only for government security budgets at police level, but also for corporate security. Local and multinational companies will need to budget for security on a long-term basis, if they are to minimize the impact of bombers, kidnappers, and conceivably assassins.

There are other regions of Europe where in the past decade nationalist minorities have to a much lesser extent exhibited tendencies to resort to violence in pursuit of autonomy or separatism. Wales, Scotland and Brittany spring to mind, yet in none of these regions, despite employment difficulties, have nationalists been so frustrated as to cause young bloods to take up arms in any number. Judged largely on recent past showing it seems improbable that these regions will display in the late 1980s the harsh characteristics of ethnic revolt, or even that the isolated acts of terrorism which occurred in the mid-1980s will grow in incidence.

Nor will the islanders of Madeira and the Azores again resort to violence in seeking independence from Lisbon, unless Portugal's government improbably falls once more into the hands of the ultra-left, as it did for a time in the mid-1970s. Then, a conservative reaction took place in the islands, as indeed occurred in northern Portugal, with all the prospects of the counter-revolution resorting to terrorism.

Significant numbers of Canary Islanders are hardly likely to be tempted into supporting the Movement for the Self-Determination and Independence of the Canary Islands Archipelago (MPAIAC), which has claimed the isolated explosion. Nor is there much prospect of a serious challenge to the unity of Italy from Sardinian separatists, though they may emulate criminals and resort to kidnapping.

On the other hand, a region which might well prove problematic is Catalonia, where nationalist sentiment is on the make. True, by 1984, Free Land (TL) had made little impact with its isolated bombings, but the danger could arise from a talented, experienced and wealthy provincial government deciding democratically to withdraw from the Spanish State. Local police would find it impossible to resist martial law once it had been imposed, some nationalists would undoubtedly resort to clandestine activities resulting in terrorist acts. It is impossible to determine the probability of such a scenario; suffice it to say that it cannot be discounted. In the event the terrorists would target security force facilities and possibly representatives of central government, and in addition non-Catalan Spanish banks.

Belgium offers disquieting prospects thanks to the national divide between French and Flemish speakers. Though communal violence in the form of riots will on occasions flare up, sustained terrorism resulting from a campaign organized by a group or groups of nationalists seems an unlikely prospect.

IDEOLOGICAL TERRORISM

Germany and Italy were worst affected by the new leftist ideas which arose from the student revolution of 1968. Such groups as the Red Army Faction (RAF) and the Red Brigades (BR) emerged from a so-called autonomy movement which saw itself to the left of the orthodox communist parties. Police action, following an immense national effort, got the better of the phenomenon. Neither democratic Germany nor democratic Italy could comprehend why it was that in times of national prosperity and constitutionally enshrined individual liberties the children of democracy should reject freedoms established on the ashes of fascist regimes. But so it was.

Both states misread the problem, and failed to see that what the security forces took to be a series of incidents was in fact a cleverly devised campaign to undermine the authority of the state. Systematically the pillars of the establishment were attacked by the intimidation through terrorism of a few representatives of the educational system, the media, the judiciary, quasi-state corporations and the Christian Democratic Party. The police approach to solving each incident was the same as that towards solving common crime: no perception of linkage existed, nor was the machinery of law and order constructed to detect linkage, let alone operate in a manner likely to combat the problem effectively. All manner of local jurisdictions had to be revised, police forces had to learn to cooperate with one another nationally and internationally, new special units had to be set up and their responsibilities clearly established. The terrorist phenomenon in Italy and Germany therefore transformed the security systems of these countries, leaving them in a strong position to handle any re-emergence.

It seems unlikely that the strategy of armed struggle or, as the RAF put it, the long march through the institutions, will again be resorted to, at least in the medium term (three to five years). The reasons are that in Germany, the RAF was revealed as an arrogant elitist organization, inward looking, concerned with itself rather than society. But worst for its morale, the RAF failed, and today a new phenomenon is at work, that of the Revolutionary Cells (RZ) which operates loosely, at parochial levels. In Italy the leadership of BR and related organizations such as Front Line (PL) abandoned the armed struggle from their prison cells in 1982. Defeat compelled them to re-examine their strategy, though imprisonment has not shaken their revolutionary ardour. They remain opposed to democratic consensus government. Their ability to put that opposition into practice through terrorism is reduced because the strategy has lost credibility on the ultra-left and because the security institutions of the state are geared to understanding and handling the matter.

Other countries suffered from the reverberations of 1968, but not to the same extent. In France, where the Gaullist Fifth Republic was on the point of falling, the ultra-left did not see the need to resort to clandestinely organized terrorist acts. That said, ten years later Direct Action (AD) irritates the Mitterand Administration by attacking French foreign policy, particularly towards Africa, through exploding bombs in or near Defence Ministry buildings. The group exhibits hostility towards Israel and the US, whose consular and diplomatic facilities are at risk from its bombings, as is American business. Arrests of leaders in March 1984 made little difference to AD's bombing of defence-related establishments. Indeed the October 1984 emergence in Belgium of attacks on defence-related industry suggested that AD tactics would not in future be confined to France.

The Spanish left in the 1970s was looking towards Franco's death (1975), and terrorism was attractive only to a handful of militants on the Maoist fringe, which spawned both the Anti-Fascist and Patriotic Revolutionary Front (FRAP), now defunct, and the First of October Anti-Fascist Resistance Group (GRAPO). Despite police successes against GRAPO, the group still poses a security problem in the mid-1980s. There appears to be central direction to regional committees, judging from the simultaneous actions in far-flung cities of the realm that occasionally occur. GRAPO is markedly anti-capitalist in its ideology and quite ruthlessly targets local businessmen, whom it duns for revolutionary taxes. The year 1984 saw the group acting in solidarity with ETA by attacking French industrial concerns, which bore the brunt of France's decision to extradite Spanish Basque terrorists to stand trial in Madrid. In future GRAPO could well turn its attention to foreign business.

Elsewhere in Europe, ideological terrorism played little or no part in political violence during the 1970s, and nothing indicates that it will do so in the 1990s. The re-emergence of Otelo Saraiva de Carvalho in Portugal as a possible instigator of FP25's occasional bomb attacks against local business targets is an exception to the rule, but will prove transitory in nature. The indicators of trouble brewing in Portugal will be seen in Spain first, since Lusitanian disturbances almost invariably follow Spanish unrest.

INTERNATIONAL TERRORISM

Because of its involvement in world affairs and its liberal traditions, Europe will always attract exiles. Unscrupulous states, such as those ruled by Gaddafi or Khomeini, will seek them out, so that European states will continue to suffer from political conflicts and disputes to which it is not a party. Moreover Arab regimes which reject any form of accommodation with Israel will harbour Palestinian groups that are prepared to operate overseas and will, as does Iraq, use them to promote their own foreign policy interests. If at any point these interests conflict with those of Europe these states are and will continue to be prepared to resort to clandestine acts to achieve their designs. Britain, as the seizure of the Iranian Embassy in 1980 and the firing of machine-guns by diplomatic staff from the windows of the 'Libyan People's Bureau' at street demonstrators in London in 1984 have shown, is not protected by its insularity, though it is hard to imagine such incidents affecting the corporate world. Nonetheless, where evidence of alliance, kinship or support for the enemy can, however improperly, be deduced, the corporation could find itself the object of attack in an attempt to cause it to desist or change its trading pattern or policy.

Solidarity is important to terrorist groups, which may act on each other's behalf, so that linkage is an essential concept to monitor. Developments could include the extension to

European territory of the Kurdish struggle for national recognition and the Baluch and Azerbaijani issues.

ENVIRONMENTALIST TERRORISM

In West Germany RZ established autonomously organized nuclei in factories and universities in the mid-1970s, when they hoped to build up revolutionary counter power. Their bomb targets are chiefly establishments which to them represent 'imperialism' and 'Zionism', so that the defence industry and American and Israeli premises are at risk. Cumulatively the destructive effect of bombing is supposed to lay the basis for 'mass perspective'. Many of their attacks take place on industrial property, largely concentrated on the Frankfurt–Wiesbaden area, Berlin, and the Ruhr, but a principal target remains US, German and British military facilities.

More recently RZ activity has embraced opposition to local projects, controversial for their impact on the environment. One celebrated example has been the extension of the Frankfurt airport runway: the headquarters of companies involved in the construction were attacked and sabotage of the work site has been attempted. More broadly RZ is hostile towards the US for its involvement in Central America, and is against the development of civilian nuclear power. In 1983 it adopted a stance against the Turkish military regime, and there were indications in 1984 that companies operating in the Third World, where they could be accused of exploitation, would suffer bomb attacks. Attacks are made either with explosives or through arson: the vast majority of fires are unclaimed but those who engage in these actions are, at least, sympathetic to RZ, and do so as part of a 'guerrilla dispersion' strategy. Their targets are banks, public utilities, the nuclear industry and commerce and descend to irritating levels of amateur harassment, such as glueing up locks and turning on fire sprinklers to ruin merchandise.

Italian ultra-leftists, who contributed original and imaginative political analysis in the 1970s, are not prone in the mid-1980s to translate their undoubted awareness of international developments into terrorist attacks on industry. Such a development could occur in the late 1980s, especially if they have any regard for the success of RZ in Germany, where the police have difficulty in countering the activities of part-time terrorists who form a gang for one particular action and then revert to their normal employment.

Whether such a development will occur only time will tell, but issues such as nuclear power and nuclear arms are not confined by national boundaries. The danger exists that even countries like Switzerland, or indeed Denmark, Norway and Sweden, hitherto largely immune from terrorist incidents, could become the scene for protests and direct action, within the spectrum of which sabotage and terrorist actions could occur. Already Swiss society has seen sabotage against nuclear power installations, and on one isolated occasion the Pilatus aircraft factory was targetted, allegedly for selling to Central America aircraft that are used for counter-insurgency purposes.

The late 1980s will see different issues coming to the fore, and they will affect companies and governments equally. Furthermore they too will not be confined by state frontiers. The extent to which laws will be broken depends partly upon the legitimacy of the grievance and whether reform can reasonably accommodate the demands, and partly upon the extent to which agitators, intent upon broadening support for their own minority political views by demonstrating solidarity, infiltrate such movements. This is common and obvious policy, and is best demonstrated by observing the way in which ETA opposes the development of nuclear power in the Basque country. Feeling its support declining, ETA decided to stop the construction of the nuclear power plant at Lemoniz by murdering first the chief engineer and then his successor, thereby hoping to align the substantial anti-nuclear movement with ETA's separatist designs.

It is not far-fetched to see in the late 1980s the projection of animal liberation across boundaries. The use of animals for experimental purposes by hospitals and pharmaceutical companies is already controversial in Britain, the Netherlands and Germany, where direct action has led to the interruption of experiments which may take years to complete and which are costly and time-consuming to restart. Following the establishment of its philosophical foundations in the early 1970s, the movement's politicization is already well under way. The issue will grow as slogans such as 'Every burger means a murder' brings militant vegetarianism into the folds of animal liberation, whose activities will become more radical as the hard core ultra-left sidles up to the sentimentalists. Corporations will need to look at the implications of the animal liberation movement on sales, whilst police and security directors will be confronted by problems of increasingly well planned direct action involving mass trespass, breakage and entry, stealing of documents, harassment of key individuals and actual sabotage. As unemployment grows throughout Europe and leisure time expands, young people will be at risk from pressure groups anxious to recruit and so to promote causes, and willing to push the limits of their activities beyond the law.

10 North Africa and the Middle East

ALISON CONNORTON

Most political violence in the Middle East and North Africa is motivated by ethnic feeling or Islamic fundamentalism, the fervour of which is likely to increase rather than diminish over the next ten years. Militant Islam (see below) is no new phenomenon to the Muslim world; what distinguishes the fundamentalist revival of the 1980s is that, under Iranian guidance, the movement has become a Shia 'crusade', in whose name spectacular acts of international terrorism are committed against both Western and pro-Western Arab targets. The purpose is to spread the Islamic revolution and expel Western influence. By contrast, most militant ethnic groups, for example Kurdish rebels, have the more limited aim of achieving some degree of autonomy. They direct violence mainly at the regimes blocking this achievement, and the struggle is rarely carried out internationally. The obvious and notorious exception is the Palestine Liberation Organisation (PLO).

THE PALESTINE LIBERATION ORGANIZATION

In the 18 months following the Israeli invasion of Lebanon, it almost looked as if Israel had achieved its principal objective – the destruction of the PLO in Lebanon. Without a base or weapons, with thousands of guerrillas dispersed throughout the Arab world, and with bitter quarrels amongst those who remained, PLO terrorist operations against Israel declined significantly. There was a rash of solidarity attacks by, amongst others, French, Greek and Latin American terrorist groups against Israeli and Jewish targets around the world as the PLO called in 'debts', but by the end of 1982 repayment had largely been made.

In fact, the bitter blow dealt to the movement in Lebanon and the rifts in the PLO which followed radicalized some of the Palestinian fedayeen organizations which in recent years had refrained from international terrorism or used it sparingly and almost exclusively against Jewish–Israeli targets. Frustration over recent events in Lebanon and, on a practical level, new-found Syrian sponsorship, inclined the groups rejecting any form of accommodation with Israel to move once more towards terrorism.

The greatest single threat comes from Abu Nidal's Revolutionary Council Black June Organisation, a renegade Palestinian faction which has kept up a sustained terrorist campaign with the close backing first of Iraq and now of Syria against Israeli and Jewish targets (outside Israel), Arab moderate states and pro-Arafat PLO representatives, and which could turn against Western interests.

With the revival in the fortunes of the rejectionist groups' terrorist attacks are once again being launched into Israel from re-established PLO bases in Syrian-controlled areas of Lebanon. Since February 1984 there have been five major PLO attacks in Israel, and countless small-scale attacks and foiled operations. Disturbing features of some of the new operations are their boldness and almost suicidal quality. On 2 April 1984, three Democratic Front terrorists opened fire in a crowded street in Jerusalem and lobbed hand grenades amongst terrified shoppers. One terrorist was killed in a hail of return fire and the two others were arrested. Only days later four Popular Front guerrillas hijacked an Israeli bus en route to Ashkelon and held 35 passengers hostage. Soldiers stormed the bus and all four terrorists died.

The 1984 attacks demonstrate a Palestinian determination to centre the struggle inside Israel though attacks against Arab targets perceived as too moderate have not been abandoned. In recent months numerous bombings in Jordan, attacks on Jordanian diplomats in Rome, Madrid, Athens and New Delhi and the assassination of the UAE Ambassador in Paris have all been attributed to Palestinian groups. The PLO will continue to use terrorism in relentless pursuit of its political goals.

Future peace initiatives felt by the rejectionist PLO factions to be unfavourable or too concessionary towards Israel will provoke attack. As long as Egypt maintains the peace treaty with Israel, Arab re-acceptance of Egypt will meet with violent opposition. The danger further exists that violence could be directed against Western countries who closely and publicly associate with Egypt, Jordan and others that break the rejectionist ranks in future; or against countries who have first-hand involvement in peace initiatives. The assassination of a British diplomat in Athens in March 1984 at a time when the UK was seen to be forging even closer links with Jordan is a taste of what is to come.

The threat is primarily to diplomatic personnel but to discourage all-important trade links, terrorists may turn on Western commercial interests. In the heyday of Palestinian terrorism, there were few attacks on commerce primarily because bombs against banks and factories do not make banner headlines and at that time international PLO operations – hijackings, embassy sieges, the Munich Olympics – had one dominant aim: publicity. So much has changed that it is hard to envisage the need for a return to those spectacular forms of publicity-seeking terrorism. However, tactics along the lines of the Shia terrorists' high casualty truck bombs, which were apparently so successful in driving the American presence out of Lebanon, may prove irresistibly attractive.

The new PLO terrorist campaign will be primarily directed against Israeli diplomatic and high profile commercial targets and Zionist personalities and organizations. US diplomatic and high profile commercial targets also are at risk, as are the diplomatic representatives of moderate Arab states.

Further attacks will reflect Syrian policy and the extent to which Syria can now manipulate certain Palestinian groups, ostensibly to further the Palestinian cause but more accurately to serve her own political ends in the same way as Iran exploits Middle Eastern Shia groups.

The resurgence of international Palestinian terrorism supported by Syria will undoubtedly be accompanied by renewed cooperation between militant PLO groups and foreign terrorist groups. The Armenian group ASALA, the Turkish

People's Liberation Army (TPLA), Direct Action in France and the Italian Red Brigades are all groups with past Palestinian connections which could again be useful allies in the future, and Palestinian contacts extending to Latin America and even South Africa may be revived.

The tragedy of the Palestinians is that they are an ethnic group deprived of a homeland; the tragedy of ethnic groups like the Kurds, the Baluchis and the Azerbaijanis is that modern frontiers have split their homelands and totalitarian or authoritarian regimes have attempted to suppress their cultures. None of these people fight as a united movement but the national elements have all produced local resistance groups which constitute a serious domestic cross-border destabilizing threat. The problem is nowhere more graphically illustrated than in Kurdistan.

THE KURDS

Kurdistan extends over South-Eastern Turkey, North-Eastern Iraq and North-Western Iran. Kurdish nationalist movements in all three countries are strong and militant. Although in principle the Kurdish movements seek autonomy through peaceful agreement, repressive regimes have stimulated armed resistance. The attitude of the ruling regime towards its Kurdish community at any one time tends to dictate the level of resistance activity.

The Kurds have long been both a thorn in the sides of Tehran and Baghdad and also a useful tool in the many conflicts between the two countries. In the present war both Iran and Iraq have made conciliatory gestures towards their own Kurdish rebels – the Kurds might not fight with them, but they might be persuaded not to fight against them. Only Iraq has met with any success. President Saddam Hussein arranged a ceasefire with one of Iraq's principal Kurdish opposition movements, the Patriotic Union of Kurdistan (PUK) and an agreement is hoped for. The ceasefire does not include the Kurdish Democratic Party-Iraq (KDP-IRAQ), who, with Iranian support, continue to fight the Iraqi regime, not just for autonomy but for the overthrow of Saddam Hussein.

The KDP-IRAQ abduct foreigners in Iraqi Kurdistan for

publicity and to discourage overseas companies from engaging in development projects such as water supply and construction, which they regard as a part of Baghdad's 'Arabizing' policy. The hostages, mostly Western Europeans, are also part of a KDP attempt to extort the release of about 60 political prisoners, and the repatriation of Kurds ejected from Kurdistan by the Iraqi authorities. Kidnapping of expatriate technicians working on development projects in Kurdistan will continue.

In Iran Kurdish rebel groups do not threaten foreign business; their fight is solely against the Khomeini regime, which has launched an all-out offensive to crush resistance and is planning to control the Kurdish problem by the forced relocation of thousands of villagers from the Sardasht region. The bitterness that such a move would create would prolong the Kurdish struggle. Ruthless action by the Turkish government also has ensured the continuation of Kurdish rebellion. The Turkish government refuses to acknowledge Kurdish identity and has responded to resistance by sealing off the region, imprisoning large numbers of activists and launching military offensives against the rebels. With Iraqi approval, Turkish troops have pursued rebels across the border where they have established bases.

The Kurdish protest outside Kurdistan is relatively peaceful and confined to European countries. Turkish and Iranian Kurds have demonstrated outside and occupied their national embassies in Paris and The Hague. It is quite possible, however, that these groups will in future resort to terrorist tactics in Europe.

IRAN'S OTHER MINORITIES

Iran also has two other militant ethnic minorities to contend with: the Baluch and the Azerbaijanis. Of the two, the Baluch are more active.

To some extent bought off with development projects by the Shah, the Baluch nationalist movement was stirred into action by the Islamic revolution. Economic aid to the area dried up, added to which Khomeini offers no better prospect of autonomy than did the Shah; furthermore the Sunni Baluch are apprehensive of the regime's Shia emphasis. Active resistance is limited at present to occasional ambushes of military vehicles in the Zahidan area. On a number of occasions, most recently during the elections in April 1984, Baluchi resentment has flared up in the larger provincial towns. A government crackdown on drug smuggling in Baluchistan on both sides of the Iran–Pakistan border – a traffic to which the Shah had turned a blind eye – will increase support for the Baluch resistance movement.

Whilst ethnic groups are a severely disruptive influence, not least because they can so easily be a weapon in the hands of a hostile neighbour, the size of the resistance groups and the lack of unity amongst them makes them less of a challenge to the stability of the regimes than might appear.

There are two other important ethnic groups worthy of mention but their nature sets them apart: Western Saharans and Armenians.

POLISARIO

Guerrillas of the Popular Front for the Liberation of Saguia El Hamra and Rio de Oro, known as POLISARIO, are fighting a ten-year-old war with Morocco for control of the former Spanish territory of the Western Sahara. The guerrillas' political front, the Saharan Arab Democratic Republic, is recognized by 27 states but the fact that many of the fighters and refugees apparently seeking respite from the war in Algeria do not originate from the Spanish Sahara, diminishes the justification for the struggle.

The war between POLISARIO and Morocco, which has affected every country in the Mahgreb, is the greatest potential source of instability in the region. The war has been in stalemate since 1981, when Morocco pulled back into the 'useful triangle' defended by desert earthworks but POLISARIO guerrillas, armed and supported by Algeria, have kept up their harassment of Moroccan forces. Morocco in turn continues to extend the defensive desert earthworks in an attempt to stop guerrilla movement between the Tindouf area of Algeria and the south, and has poured in more than 30 000 troops to the main trouble spot around Zag near the Tindouf border area. The military commitment and the surprise treaty of union signed in August 1984 with Libya, a POLISARIO supporter, underline

Moroccan determination to retain the Western Sahara and the lucrative Bu Craa phosphate mines at all costs.

In the past POLISARIO has shied away from terrorism, but Spaniards have been abducted in order to pressurize Spain into recognizing POLISARIO. It is conceivable that other foreigners – aid workers and businessmen – also will be threatened by abduction. Shipping, particularly fishing vessels, also is at some risk off the Atlantic coast, though in general terrorism as a tactic is perceived by the SADR, POLISARIO's political front, as likely to undermine its hard-won recognition.

POLISARIO has been consistent throughout the conflict in its attempts to stop foreign exploitation of the Western Sahara's national resources. This has been taken to justify attacks against the foreign fishing fleets. On land, an effective exclusion zone may limit POLISARIO to frontal attacks on the wall, which it must penetrate if it is to renew attempts to disrupt phosphate mining. Future targets could include production and transportation facilities: in April 1984 POLISARIO claimed a successful commando raid on La'youn port, the phosphate rock outlet inside the defensive earthworks. Attacks could again spill over into the state of Morocco where, as in the past, military garrisons would be attacked rather than civilian or business targets. So long as Algeria continues to support POLISARIO there will be no need for the movement to resort to attempted kidnaps of businessmen for ransom or to levy so-called revolutionary taxes on business anxious to avoid bomb attacks on premises.

Morocco's refusal to acknowledge the validity of the SADR claim to the territory or to negotiate with POLISARIO will ensure a continuation of the conflict. For the immediate future, POLISARIO's main supporter, Algeria, is not seeking to escalate the conflict and will not tangle militarily with Morocco; looking further ahead the strains that the dispute imposes on regional relationships could cause wider conflict but the damage inflicted is likely to be sudden and over a short period: national boundaries will not be modified.

ARMENIAN TERRORISM

Armenian terrorists in 1975 began in earnest a campaign of brutal attacks on Turkish diplomats in Europe and America in revenge for the 1915 genocide of the Armenian people in Turkey. Extremists from the Armenian Secret Army for the Liberation of Armenia (ASALA), the Justice Commandos for the Armenian Genocide (JCAG) and the Armenian Revolutionary Army operate for the most part out of Lebanon. In the past ASALA has staged retaliatory attacks against other countries, for instance, France and Switzerland, for imprisoning fellow terrorists or for supporting Turkey, and may do so again.

Armenian terrorists, because they have no base, require sponsors and terrorist sponsors demand payment in kind. Future Armenian targets will therefore reflect the political designs of their backers. These include the Soviet Union, Syria, Iraq, Libya and possibly Iran. ASALA at present enjoys some unofficial Iranian support and may, at a future date, be required to repay the debt by promoting Iranian terrorist aims. This could lead to Armenian attacks on US and French diplomatic and commercial interests.

MILITANT ISLAM: IRAN'S SUPPORT AND INSPIRATION

State support, frequently self-interested, for the ethnic struggle is a well-established phenomenon: Arab state support for the PLO is just one element, albeit a large one, of the wider Arab–Israeli conflict; Iran and Iraq almost instinctively resort to the Kurdish weapon; and Iran has been able to turn the tap of Armenian terrorism on and off as relations with Turkey blow hot and cold. But a factor which will give new significance to the state role in the 1980s and 1990s is the Iranian revolution and the spread of Islamic revivalism throughout the Middle East and North Africa.

The Shia-led Iranian Islamic revolution has been the direct cause of the spectacular rise of Shia terrorism in recent years. Its militant, expansionist ideas and the stunning example of the victory over the Shah's regime in Iran have inspired the Shia communities elsewhere, while the activity of Iranian agents and the continuous flow of propaganda and logistic support from Tehran have been instrumental in establishing militant Shia fundamentalist groups in other Middle Eastern countries, particularly Lebanon.

Through these groups, Iran has attempted to subvert other states in the Gulf, exploiting the local Shia community. The impact is most noticeable in Kuwait, which suffered from dramatic bombings in December 1983, after which many Iranians were expelled. Infiltrators have been picked up also in the UAE. Bahrain too has been a target for Iranian subversion and Iran has backed Shia terrorist groups operating inside Iraq. Furthermore, clandestine attempts to organize revolutionary fundamentalist Shia groups have been exposed in Turkey, Saudi Arabia and Tunisia. So far, almost all Shia terrorist operations have been in the Middle East, but Iran is promoting subversion in Asian and African Muslim countries and has reportedly been recruiting among Muslims as far afield as France, Britain, Italy, Austria, and the US and groups are certainly active in France, Spain and West Germany. However, the main thrust of Shia terrorism will continue to be directed at countries with large Shia populations and close to Iran geographically: Iraq, the Gulf States and Saudi Arabia. Pacification of the internal Lebanese conflict might be expected to intensify the Iranian-sponsored terrorist effort in the Gulf and once the Iran–Iraq war is ended, an all-out offensive to turn the Gulf States into revolutionary Islamic republics is not impossible.

To date the preferred targets of Shia terrorists have been state personnel and facilities, including US and French nationals. Attacks on commercial targets have been few. If Iraq seriously damages Iranian oil production or export or there is a significant Iranian setback in the war, attacks on companies selling Iraq war materials and weapons or on Western oil interests could occur. After the war, if Iran is in a position to step up the terrorist drive against the Gulf States, Western business personnel and facilities could become the main targets, mostly because of their economic importance but also because they represent 'corrupting' Western influence.

Shia terrorists, working under the umbrella name Islamic Jihad, have caught the world's attention by the use of spectacular suicide bombings. More spectacular attacks employing large amounts of explosives and multiple concurrent assaults can be expected. Suicide terrorists, however, will be used sparingly and for major targets only. Because of the spectacular arrival of Shia terrorists on the Middle Eastern scene, the violent activities of other Islamic fundamentalist movements, prompted by the Iranian Islamic revolution if not actually promoted by Iran, have tended to be overlooked. A Sunni Muslim group seeking to impose a Khomeini-style regime in Egypt was responsible for the assassination of President Sadat in 1981. The Westernized, secular regimes of Tunisia, Algeria and Morocco, visualizing similar problems, have tried to smother the flames of Islamic fundamentalism. And even Syria, though prepared to tolerate and utilize Shia terrorists to achieve short-term advantages, ruthlessly suppressed its own Muslim Brotherhood movement. There is much fertile ground in the Middle East and North Africa in which Iran can and will sow its violent seed.

OTHER STATE SUPPORT

Iran's overriding and long-term aim is the spread of the Islamic Revolution across the Muslim world, and her sponsorship of terrorism is to that end. Syria, Iraq and Libya meanwhile promote state sponsorship of terrorist groups for opportunistic purposes.

Syrian sponsorship of Shia terrorist operations will last as long as the Lebanese crisis remains unresolved. Syria vies for dominance in Lebanon and Shia terrorism has proved to be an effective instrument in weakening the will of other competitors for influence in Lebanon – the US, France and Israel to maintain their positions there. Syria also approves of Shia terrorist activity against Iraq and Turkey, countries with which she is at odds for different reasons.

Within the PLO, Syria is backing radicals who rebelled against the leadership of Yasser Arafat and lends support to the renegade Abu Nidal's Black June organization. Syria also provides support for an alliance of dissident Baathists and Kurds operating against the Iraqi regime, and the Armenian Secret Army for the Liberation of Armenia (ASALA) is believed to receive training in camps near the Turkish frontier and in Syrian-occupied Lebanon.

Traditionally Iraq has supported terrorism, but the debilitating war with Iran and the desire to win Western support have caused the Iraqi authorities to circumscribe the activities, but not terminate the presence, of terrorists on Iraqi soil. Two

Palestinian groups supported by Baghdad are Black June and the 15 May Arab Organization for the Liberation of Palestine, which have been and could again be used by Iraq to promote its own interests overseas. Terrorism from this quarter mainly affects the governments of moderate Arab states and not international business operations.

Libya's interests in supporting terrorism coincide with Iran's in the main targets. Both countries view the US, France and Israel as their enemies and resent Western influence in general, and both oppose moderate Arab regimes. At present, Libyan involvement in Shia terrorism is apparently limited to minor assistance in arms supply and possibly some monetary aid to Shia militants in Lebanon. Libya has tried to support fundamentalist terrorist groups in Egypt, has encouraged Palestinians in Lebanon rebelling against the leadership of Yasser Arafat and was probably responsible for the mining of the Red Sea in August 1984. Such covert activities will continue into the late 1980s.

11   Africa South of the Sahara

DAVID FANTHORPE

The threats to their operations which businesses face in sub-Saharan Africa are not those of a classic terrorist kind, for the simple reason that terrorism, as we understand and suffer it in Western Europe, is not prevalent there. Rather it is the incidence of civil war and tribal conflicts, and the activities of guerrilla armies opposed to the existing government, which create hazards for companies, particularly those based outside major cities. The causes of tensions within states are naturally diverse, but without straining too hard to place countries into categories, it is possible to discern similar patterns within certain regions of sub-Saharan Africa. This survey therefore assesses firstly the threat to business posed by political instability and conflict in the least stable regions of Africa; and then examines in some detail the two tactics most frequently employed by guerrillas and which most often damage business – kidnapping and sabotage.

Within the confines of this survey it is not possible to mention, let alone discuss, every country of interest. Zaire, for example, though frequently subjected to political risk analysis, can have no more than a passing reference, despite some perspectives meriting fuller treatment. Perhaps the only certainty in a sea of possibilities is that Mobuto Sese Seko will keep his balancing-act on the tight rope into the 1990s.

113

SOUTHERN AFRICA

The most conflict-ridden area of Africa is the South, and there is every indication that it will remain so. Conflict between states arises from the abhorrence which her neighbours have for South Africa's system of racial separate development and from their consequent support for the terrorist group which appears most likely to end that system: the African National Congress (ANC). South Africa on the other hand sees her neighbours harbouring ANC terrorists, and following terrorist attacks from time to time takes reprisals. More insidiously, the Republic foments instability in neighbouring countries, in order to discourage support for the ANC. In this way South Africa exploits the racial and political weaknesses of the newly independent, post-colonial states around her.

South Africa's policy in southern Africa is bent upon self-defence. One aim is to recreate the 'cordon sanitaire' once formed by white rule in Rhodesia and Portuguese colonialism in Angola and Mozambique. This policy, which envisages a series of security pacts with adjacent states, was first openly acknowledged when the Nkomati accord was concluded with Mozambique in March 1984, though a secret pact had already been concluded with Swaziland in 1982. Such a course demands a high level of involvement in the internal affairs of Angola and Mozambique in particular, but also in Lesotho, Zimbabwe and Swaziland. It goes beyond merely prohibiting sanctuary for the ANC to dictating foreign policy alignment and even economic policy. Because of the Republic's overwhelming economic preponderance in the region the policy could succeed. Whilst the 'domino theory' holds some attractions (first Angola and Mozambique, then Rhodesia, next, surely, South Africa?) in fact South Africa is a regional Superpower. This reality will shape her actions over the next decade, and will undoubtedly lead her, whatever concessions may eventually be made in Namibia, to intervene extensively in others' affairs until she no longer fears the outside exploitation of her own internal problem.

Other states will suffer from conflict without outside interference. In Angola, the UNITA (National Union for the Total Independence of Angola) movement of Jonas Savimbi, though heavily backed by the Republic, enjoys a momentum of its own which will permit it to survive even if abandoned by its new sponsor. Apart from having a charismatic 'Africanist' leader, UNITA has a firm basis of support in the Ovimbundu people of the central highlands, which is Angola's largest ethnic group (some 40 per cent of the population); it only lost out to the ruling MPLA (Popular Movement for the Liberation of Angola) when Soviet backing at a crucial stage of the civil war ensured success to the Soviet candidate. UNITA's objective is to force the MPLA to form a government of national unity, independent of outside powers. Even if UNITA fails to achieve this aim before South African support is withdrawn or scaled down, backing will be received from other African states and elsewhere, much of it channelled through Kinshasa. Savimbi has been fighting since 1966 and there is nothing which the Cubans can do on behalf of the MPLA which UNITA has not already successfully countered in its struggle against the Portuguese.

The Mozambique National Resistance (RNM) cannot claim as distinguished a record, indeed its very existence depended upon South Africa, who took it over from the Rhodesian Central Intelligence Organisation in 1980. That RNM never established a substantial level of support amongst the rural population is of no importance, nor is the signing of any agreement between the RNM and FRELIMO: its future quite simply depends upon clandestine support from the Republic. The RNM will continue to provide South Africa with a means of controlling Mozambican policy. That said, dialogue with the Republic must be seen to produce tangible results for Maputo, since the Nkomati agreement has already provoked tensions within the ruling Politburo. The maintenance of a carefully preserved consensus will prove difficult.

By acting as go-between in FRELIMO–RNM talks, South Africa revealed its hand in Mozambique; in Zimbabwe its role has been more covert. There is little doubt that Ndebele dissidents have received training in South Africa, and aid appears at present to be channelled through Francistown in Botswana. Here again South Africa is simply exploiting the frustration which many Ndebele feel at the dominance of the Shona-speaking tribes in government, and the disappointment of former members of Joshua Nkomo's guerrilla army, who found that the Zimbabwe for which they had fought could not offer them a job – or a war. In the ZANU (Zimbabwe African

National Union) government's declared purpose of introducing one-party government lie the seeds of continuing rebellion by groups of Ndebele.

Conflict in these countries affects business very specifically (see Tactics below) beyond creating a dangerous overall security situation. In South Africa the future threat stems not from rural insurgency, but from urban attacks against finance and banking institutions and infrastructural targets. The ANC has said it will target foreign business, though no campaign had resulted by 1984. The ANC may wait to fulfil this warning until it can be coordinated with a campaign of large-scale industrial unrest, but it must be taken as a serious possibility within the next ten years. Such a coordinated campaign seems the best hope for the ANC to disrupt the process of gradual reform which P. W. Botha has undertaken.

EAST AFRICA

East Africa is, by and large, a model of stability in comparison with the South, but there are latent weaknesses which could surface in the next ten years. Two of these apply more or less generally throughout the region: how to ensure a smooth succession to the second generation of post-colonial leaders (a problem, indeed, in many parts of Africa), and how to reconcile the conflicting aspiration of different tribal groups, often with a history of mutual antagonism.

Kenya is illustrative of both these problems, and suffers, additionally, from a third: a rapid rate of population growth (some 4 per cent per annum) that is the highest in the world. Enlightened and far-seeing leadership will be necessary simply to feed the burgeoning population, but perhaps even more appalling are the potential social problems. Nairobi's shanty-towns will continue to expand, housing many unemployed, and becoming breeding-grounds for still more violent crime. The emergence of skilled leadership will be accidental; already two attempts have been made to remove President Daniel Arap Moi and he still lacks a firm grip and is greatly beholden to army leaders. In tribal politics, he has shown determination to loosen the hold which the Kikuyu had at the time of his succession, not only in KANU, the sole legal party, but also in the armed services and the civil service. Inevitably Moi's own Kalenjin tribe has benefitted, but the issue in the years to come will not be favouritism for the Kalenjin, but how the Kikuyu respond to their diminished role in national affairs.

Tribal rivalry is far more obviously the source of the horrific violence which continues to beset Uganda. The main opposition to President Milton Obote, who ousted Amin with Tanzanian help, came from the Baganda, many of whom, when democratic opposition seemed to be a dead letter after disputed elections in 1980, gave support to a guerrilla leader, Yoweri Museveni (a former defence minister), and his National Resistance Army (NRA). Amin's bloody rule contributed an element of religious persecution as well; he is himself a Muslim. Former Amin supporters are now grouping in Amin's home province, West Nile, and could prove to be the origin of yet more violence in future years.

The NRA and the Ugandan army have between them perpetrated numerous atrocities, and the NRA appear to have been responsible for the abduction, and in some cases the murder of several Europeans, including four employees of the World Bank. The NRA has long been active within only a few miles of Kampala, and the country outside the capital will be dangerous for a long time. A further threat, which finally overthrew Obote, stemmed from the rivalry even within the national army between his own Lango tribe and the Acholi.

Mention has already been made of the religious element in Amin's 1971 take-over. To the north of Uganda Muslim rivalry both with Christianity and with traditional African religions (often animist) became more acute, particularly as the boundary between the two religions lies like a spiritual San Andreas fault down the middle of several African countries.

At the eastern end of the fault-line is Sudan, a very large country which has never found it easy to remain an integrated whole. A period of peace which opened in 1972, following a 15-year civil war, came to an end in spring 1983 when southern grievances about domination from the north re-surfaced, given new impetus by the discovery of oil in the south. Southerners resented a pipeline being laid to take the oil north to Port Sudan, which appeared to add to their economic subordination. Abandoning his previously conciliatory approach, President Nimeiri added to southern fears by introducing strict Islamic

Sharia law into the north. Several Christians have fallen foul of it, including some expatriates; for example, an Italian was flogged for possessing alcohol.

The main guerrilla group fighting in southern Sudan is the Sudanese People's Liberation Army (SPLA). Its objected is southern autonomy, though many southerners would probably accept continued integration in Sudan so long as militant Islam, at present personified by Nimeiri and his advisers from the Sufi sect, are not in power in Khartoum. The inherent instability of Sudan was demonstrated when Nimeiri, sick and apparently also unstable, was ousted in April 1985. Nimeiri's successor will have to accommodate the South if civil war is to be avoided.

Sudan has long been a haven for Ethiopian refugees from the Marxist–Leninist regime in Addis Ababa. (Conversely, the SPLA operates from bases in Ethiopia.) It probably also offers some support to the northern-based separatists in Eritrea (the Eritrean People's Liberation Front (EPLF) is the most effective group) and in Tigre province (Somalia, however, provides much more extensive support to groups fighting for Somali self-determination in Ethiopia, and Ethiopia reciprocates by backing the Democratic Front for the Salvation of Somalia). The Horn of Africa has relatively little foreign business and conflict which has been endemic for years has hardly impinged on economic development; whilst a *rapprochement* between Ethiopia and Somalia is feasible, the groups fighting for autonomy in the north are likely to continue to drain Ethiopia's limited monetary resources.

WEST AFRICA

Religious divides like that in Sudan also exist in several West African countries, but there they tend rather to emphasize the diversity of a country's population, rather than in themselves act as a major cause of instability. The best example is Nigeria, a vast country with a rapidly growing population, which has tended to find leaders in the (Muslim) Hausa-Fulani aristocracy in the north, but whose business is often in the hands of non-Muslim southerners (mainly Yoruba, from the south-western states). Nigeria still hopes to find in federation the cure for the ethnic tensions which found expression in the 1967–70 civil war, but has not yet found an appropriate way to give Africa a lead in democratic government.

However, military government is now a widespread tradition in West Africa, and often the best guarantee of peace and even progress. One example is the new government of Guinea, a country kept in isolation by Sekou Toure but now being ruled by a military junta which is committed to improving the small nation's economy. Although the price that was paid may be considered heavy, Sekou Toure provided stability, and in this respect the francophone countries have generally proved more successful than the anglophone. No doubt the French ability to adapt their role from colonial master to Third World patron is part of the explanation; the fact that the oil which has cursed Nigeria has blessed Gabon may reflect the different colonial legacies.

Apart from the comings and goings of military governments, which do not always affect business, West Africa poses relatively few security problems to corporations.

TACTICS EMPLOYED AGAINST BUSINESS: KIDNAPPING AND ABDUCTION

The use of abduction by guerrilla groups has increased greatly in the 1980s so that it is now virtually the major threat to business, and there are indications that this trend will continue throughout the rest of the decade. Kidnapping for ransom is relatively rare; more often personnel are abducted as a means of gaining publicity and recognition. In two countries, Angola and Sudan, guerrillas are pursuing more sophisticated objectives: their aim is to hasten the downfall of the regime they oppose by forcing foreign business to withdraw from the country. To this end UNITA in Angola and the southern rebels in Sudan have mounted abduction campaigns.

Guerrilla demands following the abduction of foreign workers in Sudan became overtly political in November 1983. They also directly involved foreign business. In two separate actions in that month the SPLA seized foreign workers involved in oil exploration 16 miles south of Bentiu, and employees of a French construction consortium employed on the Jonglei Canal project at Malakal. Although the hostages were released after three days, the raids forced a temporary suspension of work by the companies. When some work was resumed, the guerrillas struck again in February 1984, attacking the oil company's camp and again abducting a number of French consortium's employees. Four were still held hostage in October 1984.

Again in forcing the suspension of work in the south, the SPLA has been startlingly successful both in preventing what it finds immediately objectionable – 'export' of southern revenues to the north, an affront to southern aspirations for autonomy – and also in depriving Sudan's government of oil royalties, without which a tottering economy will collapse unless supported by the US (as has already happened once). This tactic has been used with such devastating success by the SPLA that imitations of it seem inevitable; in terms of economy of guerrilla effort it is unsurpassable.

Whether further use of the tactic will be made in Sudan itself is doubtful, precisely because of the overwhelming success it has already met. The development of the southern insurgency also depends on those factors adumbrated earlier in this chapter but it could be for example that a full-scale civil war will develop, so that, as happened in El Salvador in 1980, kidnapping might become a less appropriate tactic (always supposing there were any businessmen left to abduct).

In Angola UNITA leader Jonas Savimbi has openly declared that his purpose is to force business to withdraw and so precipitate economic collapse. Overseas companies are denounced as 'collaborators' with the MPLA regime; however expatriates are treated well when captured and do not suffer personally for what Savimbi sees as the shortcomings of their governments, though the average period of detention is almost eight months. They are usually released unconditionally through the Red Cross, having given an undertaking not to return to Angola whilst the civil war continues.

Until 1983 expatriate workers were captured by UNITA guerrillas in the course of general raids throughout Angola (mostly at that time in eastern Angola and the central highlands), but during that year Savimbi announced that UNITA would make deliberate attempts to capture expatriates. One of the first faults of this policy was a raid on an outlying diamond mining town, Cafunfo, in Lunda Norte province in

February 1984, in which 77 foreigners were taken prisoner. The condition on which the 16 Britons among them were released is instructive, as are the initial UNITA demands. UNITA wanted the British government to order its nationals out of Angola, thereby crippling the diamond mines which employ considerable British expertise. Not surprisingly the British government refused, but it did assent to a UNITA proviso that the prisoners would be released only when a senior diplomat went to Angola to ask for them. As a consequence UNITA scored a resounding propaganda success when Savimbi's meeting with Sir John Leahy was widely reported in the Western media.

For all this UNITA's campaign against the MPLA, whilst gaining ground in other ways, has made very little headway in forcing business to leave. The key to this campaign is the oil industry, which is based in Cabinda and offshore. Oil provides 90 per cent of Angola's foreign exchange; diamonds and coffee, more vulnerable to UNITA raids, are minor contributors in comparison.

The next UNITA target, therefore, must be the abduction of oil industry workers, as well as sabotage (already begun – see below). As mentioned above, their captives are usually released unconditionally. However, if wider regional developments were to leave UNITA bereft of South African support, UNITA might be tempted to make material demands for the release of hostages. This is not likely over the next two years, when UNITA stockpiles and other supplies would cover any shortfall, but as a longer-term possibility it must be taken seriously into account.

Other countries in which guerrilla groups have captured expatriates include Mozambique, Zimbabwe and Uganda. Of these Zimbabwe is perhaps most likely to show an increase in kidnapping, depending on the level of insurgency in Matabeleland. However, the Mozambique National Resistance (RNM) in Mozambique, whose future is in doubt at the time of writing, could find itself pushed back into remote parts of the country, where it might adopt 'spoiling' tactics, including the abduction of expatriate workers employed on agricultural complexes or construction projects. The latter have been particular victims of RNM in the past. An increase in kidnapping in Uganda is unlikely – there the ferocity of the guerrillas, struggle with the army is more likely to lead to murder than kidnap.

In South Africa, there are no indications as yet that the ANC intends to adopt kidnapping as a tactic in its struggle against apartheid; the ANC must expect that the South African government would refuse to negotiate or allow a third party to meet demands. However, the changed security position following the Nkomati accord will force the ANC to operate on a cellular basis inside South Africa. This might make kidnapping a more attractive proposition than hitherto. The purpose of such kidnaps (of politician or businessman) would be to damage morale among the white population rather than to raise funds. With a similar objective in mind, they might choose to abduct whites living in isolated rural areas, much as the Rhodesian guerrillas did in their liberation war. In those circumstances the victims could be held in a neighbouring country, such as Lesotho or Mozambique.

TACTICS EMPLOYED AGAINST BUSINESS: SABOTAGE

Sabotage is not only the most common guerrilla tactic, it also has the most immediate impact on business. Industrial sites are blown up, or burned down; goods are destroyed in transit or delayed; the economic infrastructure is damaged, and profitable business made difficult or impossible. These are all in addition to the dangers to personnel from terrorist activity. The likelihood is that business will face these perils in even greater profusion over the next decade. Although groups devoted to single 'issues', such as the anti-nuclear lobby, ecologists, animal rights protestors and all the other elements which employ sabotage techniques in the West will naturally not afflict African societies, guerrilla groups and those fighting on behalf of minority populations will certainly become more sophisticated in their use of terrorist tactics. The special place which multinational business occupies in the developing world means that it is a particularly useful target for terrorists, because it can be used to exert pressure on governments economically. Some success in this direction has already been achieved by the SPLA in Sudan, who, combining kidnapping with attacks on company installations, have crippled the Sudanese economy. UNITA in Angola also will try to break the Angolan government in the same way, by sabotage of the all-important oil industry. An oil pipe-line was blown up in Cabinda in July 1984, surely only the first strike in a prolonged campaign.

Communications are another weak spot in many African economies; long, inefficient railways labour to move goods from the interior to ports, presenting an easy target to saboteurs. Angola's railways have been almost permanently crippled since 1970, and will remain virtually indefensible for years to come. Much the same is true of Mozambican railways. Although the government claimed that the northern lines out of Beira and Nacala had been reopened in summer 1984, the southern route from Swaziland to Maputo was shortly afterwards closed by sabotage of the track in Maputo province, with the result that the Swazi sugar crop had to be re-routed through South Africa to Richard's Bay.

A final purpose of sabotage is to lower civilian morale: guerrilla activity cut electricity to three African capitals (Luanda, Maputo and Kampala) in the space of two months in autumn 1984. The same objective is pursued in South Africa by the ANC, who have targeted oil facilities, electricity substations and power pylons. At present these attacks achieve only nuisance value, but a campaign of industrial sabotage and disruption of public utilities, coupled with large-scale bomb attacks and industrial unrest, may appear the most attractive strategy to the terrorist movement.

12 Latin America

JAMES ANDERSON

THE LATIN AMERICAN TRADITION

Throughout its history, Latin America has suffered more than its fair share of political violence and upheaval. The wars of independence, the frequent revolutions and civil and inter-state wars of the nineteenth and early twentieth centuries and the social explosions of the mid twentieth century, such as 'La Violencia' in Colombia, engendered a tradition of violence in the region. In an area characterized by low levels of education, development and communications, where personalities rather than parties have often been the predominant political forces, violent confrontation leading to chronic instability and subsequent repressive military intervention to restore order have been depressingly frequent. Costa Rica's tradition of democratic, consensus politics has been the regional exception, rather than the norm to which Western European or North American states are accustomed.

Since the 1950s, ideologically motivated guerrilla groups have entered the easily exploitable political and social arena of Latin American affairs. The success of the Cuban guerrilla campaign in 1959 introduced a new method of undermining and over-throwing the state. Since then every Latin American country except Panama and Costa Rica has experienced guerrilla activity of varying types and on differing scales. The three principal varieties of guerrilla activity, all of which may still be found in the region, have been rural guerrilla movements usually based on Che Guevara's 'foco' strategy (seen currently in Colombia and Guatemala), urban terrorism such as that in Chile and Ecuador, and most recently the more broadly based 'revolutionary nationalism', currently being experienced in Central America, particularly in El Salvador.

The Cuban model invited and continues to invite emulation, and despite the fact that only in Nicaragua in 1979 – in exceptional circumstances – has it been successfully repeated, it will continue to invite imitation in the foreseeable future. The purpose of this chapter is to examine the political, social and economic factors which can spawn revolutionary movements in the region and which can provoke political violence, either of the guerrilla variety or at other less organized or ideological levels of low-intensity conflict. Some of these factors are long-standing, others are of more recent provenance or are only now beginning to appear.

The most important of the long-standing factors is the concentration of much of the national wealth in the hands of a small, sometimes tiny, percentage of the population. Somoza in Nicaragua was the classic example, along with the Duvalier dynasty in Haiti and the so-called '14 Families' in El Salvador. Seldom have governments taken drastic measures to redress this imbalance – the young officers in El Salvador in 1979 were exceptional. Rather, ruling elites have, whenever under extreme pressure, merely granted the minimum concessions necessary to defuse the immediate problem. Thus extreme disparities of wealth and poverty remain in nearly all Latin American countries; Peru and Haiti are just the most glaring examples. Parallel with the issue of wealth is that of rigid social and class distinctions. In countries where the structure of the elite is so rigid as to preclude the entry of new social or political forces, guerrilla groups will always look for support amongst the poor whose only hope of bettering their condition will come through overthrowing existing structures. Thus Costa Rica's open and flexible society has never been plagued by indigenous terrorism, and in Colombia, where the system has opened in recent years and where upward social mobility is becoming increasingly possible – President Betancur himself is from the humblest of origins – the appeal of the guerrillas is waning.

The existence of unrepresentative, repressive governments provides a justification for guerrilla groups, and Latin America has experienced many such regimes. In this respect, however, the outlook is hopeful. In 1978, only four Latin American countries had democratically elected governments; by the mid-1980s only two – Paraguay and Chile (if Brazil and Nicaragua are given the benefit of the doubt) – did not. The regional climate now strongly favours the democratic model, and only in Peru are there indications that this trend will be reversed. The reverse of the democratic coin can have its drawbacks, however. The liberal, democratic state is by its nature more vulnerable to extremist attack than the totalitarian or authoritarian state. Unless the sociological and political conditions have changed during the period of military rule, there is a risk of guerrilla resurgence. The late 1980s could see this happening in Argentina and Uruguay.

Another long-standing cause of political violence which has affected the Caribbean is the demand for independence. By the mid-1980s this had become a marginal issue with the almost complete withdrawal of the European colonial powers from the region. Nonetheless, such demands could well grow and will continue to engender sporadic violence in Puerto Rico and in the French territories of Guadeloupe and Martinique.

Nationalism is becoming an increasingly important factor, as both politicians and guerrillas adopt an anti-foreign posture in response to events, as the Falklands War showed. This will be most strongly manifested in the region over two issues.

Firstly, there is the long-standing Latin nationalism which shows itself in 'anti-Yanqui' sentiment and opposition to US policies and preponderance in the region; this feeling will remain strong as a result of the US Administration's high profile in Central America.

Secondly, economic nationalism engendered by the regional debt crisis may well prompt guerrillas to attack foreign banks and financial institutions in an attempt to increase their popularity. As the debt burden becomes heavier, there will be an increasing tendency to blame foreigners: high US interest rates, the insensitivity of foreign banks to the region's social problems and low commodity prices in the developed world will be made the scapegoats. Economic hardship amongst the poorest sectors of the community, which is aggravated by externally imposed austerity measures, could provoke street disturbances on an unprecedented scale. The violence in the Dominican Republic in April 1984 could be repeated elsewhere if explosions of a similar intensity were to break out in Sao Paulo, Rio de Janeiro, Lima or La Paz, and the authorities could well temporarily lose control of the streets.

There is one final element in Latin American society which has, since the Spanish conquest, contained the seeds of serious violence, but which has only recently induced it in any appreciable way: ethnic resurgence, illustrated by the rise of Sendero Luminoso in Peru. Owing allegiance to no outside power, maintaining no links with guerrilla groups elsewhere and with an ideology combining hard-line Maoism with the deep-rooted traditions of Indian resistance to Spanish rule and resentment of white domination, the current guerrilla phenomenon in Peru is unique. It is perhaps the single most disturbing revolutionary development in the region in recent years, in that it is the first Latin American guerrilla group to have produced any strong response from the rural, Indian population.

Much of Sendero's thinking has been moulded by the Indian experience in Peru. The examples of the Inca agricultural cooperative communities has been a powerful influence, and leaders emphasize that the group has learnt much from the examples of Atahualpa, the last Inca emperor, and of Tupac Amaru II, the leader of Inca revolt against Spanish rule in 1780–82. It would appear that the Sendero leadership is attempting a synthesis of its own Maoist view of proletarian revolution with Inca myths connected with the conquering emperor Pachacutec and with the overthrow of the world. Most leading members are either native Quechua speakers or have learnt to speak it fluently; many have married into Indian families. Most of the group's rural activists are Indian. Feeding on the traditional Indian resentment of white and mestizo domination, Sendero considers those of Spanish descent or of mixed blood to be foreigners, and believes that the Indians should rule Peru once more as the Incas did centuries ago. Drawing as it does on a messianic pre-Columbian, Andean movement which has acquired deep roots and strong motivation which will make it harder to eradicate than if it relied solely upon its narrow political ideology. The dramatic spread of Sendero activity could provide a model of political violence for other countries which also have large and disaffected Indian communities, such as Bolivia, Brazil, Guatemala and Mexico.

FOREIGN SPONSORS AND TARGETS

In the mid-1980s leftist guerrilla groups operate extensively in Chile, Colombia, El Salvador, Guatemala and Peru, and at a lower level in Ecuador and Honduras. At the same time, rightist terrorists operate in Argentina, Bolivia, Chile, Colombia, El Salvador, Guatemala and Nicaragua. The insurgencies in Peru and the Central American countries pose by far the most serious security threats, and these are likely to remain the principal areas of political violence.

In Central America, an indigenous revolutionary process has become part of the East–West conflict, with Washington emphasizing Cuba's role in exporting revolution. Outside interference will continue to exacerbate the situation: for both Washington and Havana, Central America will remain an area of prime foreign policy concern. Cuba will remain strongly supportive of the revolutionary Sandinist regime in Nicaragua. Elsewhere, however, the Cuban profile may be lower, particularly after the set-back in Grenada, where US forces intervened to prevent the establishment of a leftist pro-Soviet regime in October 1983; for example, the erratic revolutionary regime in Surinam expelled over 100 Cubans shortly afterwards. That said, Cuban commitment to revolution in El Salvador and Guatemala will continue, and the DGI (the Cuban secret service) will maintain its efforts to promote unity and coordination amongst the Central American guerrillas. Because of the geo-political importance of the area, the tough stance adopted by the Reagan Administration will continue, reducing direct Cuban interference in Central America still further, though this alone will not provide peace.

The Sandinist regime, allied to Cuba, gives strong moral support to regional guerrilla groups. However, US pressure and growing military threats to their own revolution have forced the Sandinists to reduce their material assistance. The flow of arms to El Salvador has decreased, and assistance to guerrillas in Honduras and Guatemala has been minimal: the Sandinists are unlikely to be able to contribute significant material aid in the future.

In the mid-1980s, the US has increased its direct involvement in the Caribbean basin, most notably by the intervention to reverse political developments in Grenada in October 1983.

Pressure will continue to be applied on Nicaragua, where US support for the armed opposition includes military training in Honduras. Adverse public reaction in the US forced the Reagan Administration to suspend its financial assistance to the 'contras' during 1984, but training and support will continue with the objective of compelling change towards a multi-party system in Nicaragua.

The Peruvian guerrilla war falls into two distinct categories: a rural insurgency, conducted by all sides with a savagery previously unknown in the region, and a selective terrorist campaign in the cities. In the latter, anything representing power, class or privilege is a target: government buildings, shops, hotels, banks, restaurants, embassies, the security forces – and foreign business. Attacks on foreign business tend to be regarded as counter-productive in Latin America, though it was previously targeted in El Salvador for a short period in the late 1970s. However, extreme xenophobia and a generally iconoclastic outlook lead Sendero to regard foreign business with particular aversion. Since mid-1981, foreign companies which have suffered from the guerrillas' attentions have included Holiday Inns, Sheraton Hotels (three times), Ralston-Purina (twice), Fiat, Volvo, Sears-Roebuck department stores (three times), Peru-Helvetica (twice), Goodyear, Bayer (twice), Coca-Cola (twice), Philips, Alfa-Romeo, Aeroflot and Hitachi. Sendero's attack against Bayer in May 1983 resulted in the almost total destruction of their chemical plant, involving a loss of some $50 million.

TYPES OF VIOLENCE

The various levels of political violence throughout the region may be gauged from the scale of politically motivated killings. Political assassination is a tactic frequently employed by extremists of both left and right in El Salvador, Colombia, Guatemala and Peru. Victims are usually middle-ranking local political figures: with the exception of the Colombian Justice Minister Rodrigo Lara Bonilla in April 1984, no senior politician has been assassinated in the region since the former Nicaraguan dictator Anastasio Somoza was killed in Paraguay in 1980.

Some guerrilla groups, notably in Colombia, Guatemala and Peru, regularly 'execute' alleged informers, who are usually peasants. In El Salvador and Guatemala the rate of killings will continue at a high level. Many thousands have been murdered by death squads in the civil war in El Salvador, and in Guatemala rural killings are likely to rise again after dropping somewhat in the early 1980s. With rightist death squads and sometimes the guerrillas prepared to resort to the extermination of entire rural communities, and with few political initiatives which might offer a respite, no diminution in violence will occur.

The prospects in Peru are even worse: in the first ten months of 1984 over 3500 people died in Peru, a marked increase over the 120 in 1982 and 1000 in 1983. Still more deaths may be expected as the 1980s progress. In Colombia death squads and guerrillas account for several hundred killings a year, although the number is likely to fall in the late 1980s as a result of the amnesty process. Totals of some 50 deaths per year in Chile in the early 1980s are likely to be maintained until President Pinochet relinquishes power. In other countries death will be at a much lower level.

Apart from assassination for various reasons, Latin American guerrillas employ three main tactics: bombing, kidnapping and infrastructure sabotage. Bombing is the most frequent method of guerrilla attack in Latin America. Peru is much the worst affected country, and the only one in which foreign interests are often specifically targeted. A still higher level of bombing is expected in the future. Some 500 bombings took place in Chile in 1984, a dramatic increase over previous years and this high level will persist. Sporadic bombings will also persist in Argentina, Nicaragua and Bolivia (being the work of rightists in each case), and in Honduras, Colombia and Guatemala. They will be at a very low level indeed in Brazil, Ecuador and Panama. In the Caribbean, only Guadeloupe and Martinique may be affected by bombings. As a general rule government buildings or business premises rather than the homes of individual officials or staff members are targeted.

Concerted attacks on infrastructure remain a particular tactic of Central American guerrilla warfare, and will continue. In El Salvador, persistent attacks against buses and trains have drastically reduced transport. Similar tactics are used less frequently in Guatemala, and in both these countries and in

Peru bridge sabotage will continue to aggravate transport difficulties. Electricity supplies also are attacked regularly in Guatemala, El Salvador, Peru and Chile. In Peru and Chile sabotage may increase; it will remain at its present level in El Salvador, and should decrease in Colombia and Guatemala. At the other end of the political spectrum, sabotage by the contras in Nicaragua will remain at a high level. Other countries have been largely unaffected, and should remain so.

Colombia is the country worst affected by politically motivated kidnappings, although a lower level is expected in the future; sporadic guerrilla kidnappings will occur also in Honduras and Guatemala. In El Salvador, which suffered so badly from kidnapping in the 1970s, the insurgency has risen to the level of civil war which, requiring different tactics, has led to a marked decline in political kidnappings. In Guatemala, second only to Colombia in the number of kidnappings in the region, political kidnappings have declined as the number of criminal abductions has risen, a pattern which is also emerging in Colombia. In the 1980s, the victims of kidnappers have nearly always been local figures.

Right-wing groups frequently employ the tactic of abduction, particularly in Argentina, Colombia, El Salvador, Guatemala, Honduras and Peru. No ransom demand is made and victims – always local political activists – are usually killed. Leftist guerrillas, especially in Colombia, Peru and El Salvador, sometimes use this tactic as well; victims are usually journalists or locals such as social workers, temporarily 'borrowed' to take messages to the authorities or for publicity purposes.

THE PROSPECT

Political violence will remain an integral part of Latin American affairs for the next ten years. Guerrilla groups will present a serious security threat in Central America and Peru. In many other countries, particularly Brazil, Bolivia, Ecuador, Peru and the Dominican Republic, economic decline will provoke serious disorders such as looting, rioting, industrial militancy and so on. In neither case, however, is the existence of the state going to be threatened by political violence. Over the next ten years, Peru seems the only country in the region which could experience severe, traumatic upheaval, but Sendero Luminoso would only be part of the reason for such a collapse: a symptom of a failed social and political model rather than a cause of that failure.

Despite the severe social and economic difficulties which the region will face over the next ten years, a note of optimism seems justified. Two interlinked developments of the mid-1980s may indicate the way forward in dealing with both the region's subversive groups and its social problems: the Colombian peace process and the Contadora initiative in Central America. In the past, there was money to buy off opposition, as Venezuela did in the 1970s; now there is not. What there now *does* seem to be, however, is a willingness on all sides to see if consensus rather than confrontation can provide a better remedy for the region's social problems.

13 Asia

JOHN BRAY

Few Asian countries have remained free of serious political violence since the end of the Second World War. The Indian sub-continent is still plagued both by communal riots and by more organized secessionist movements. Burma, Thailand, Malaysia, Indonesia and the Philippines have all faced communist insurgencies and the repercussions of the Vietnam war still resound in Kampuchea. In many cases the patterns of conflict, such as the continuing struggle between lowland Burmans and the neighbouring hill peoples, can be traced back for centuries. Some of these old leitmotifs will still be discernible in the next decade, but with new variations brought by modern ideologies and fresh grievances. This chapter reviews four principal themes, often closely interlinked, which are associated with contemporary Asian political violence: urban riots, Islam, the role of secessionist movements led by ethnic minorities, and communist insurgencies.

URBAN RIOTS

'Timeless Asia' has always been a tourist brochure misnomer but the current accelerating pace of social and economic change is particularly apparent in urban areas. Asia's overcrowded cities will continue to grow rapidly until well into the next century. By the year 2000 Jakarta's population will have doubled to some 14 million and Bombay's to 16 million, 75 per cent of them slum-dwellers. Other cities throughout the region will expand at a similar rate.

Few of the millions or rural immigrants make their fortunes. Those who do not will inevitably be tempted by crime (though the main streets of most Indian cities are still safer by night than the streets of most American cities, precisely because they are more crowded). It is a measure of the desperation as well as the ruthlessness of the Indonesian regime that it has resorted to extra-legal assassination squads to deter criminals. And in Port Moresby, Papua New Guinea, for example, gangs of *raskols* ('rascals') made up of rural immigrants are responsible for an escalating violent crime rate. As society develops in this way, there is a heightened risk of communal violence in overcrowded cities. Disoriented migrants often look to religious organizations for reassurance – this is one reason for the rise in the support for militant Hindu organizations like the Rashtriya Swayamsevak Sangh (RSS) in India – and they seek scapegoats when they fall behind in the competition for scarce resources.

India's Hindus are more militant and the Muslims more assertive than at any time since independence. Hindu–Muslim riots are an ancient problem but in recent years their frequency has increased. In 1981, 196 people were killed in communal violence. In 1982 the figure rose to 238 and in 1983 to 1143. The figure for 1984 is certain to be even higher in the wake of the assault on the Sikh Golden Temple in Amritsar and the assassination of Mrs Gandhi.

Economic deprivation and religious fervour make a highly combustible mixture which is certain to produce more explosions not only in India but also in Indonesia, where Chinese businessmen are the traditional scapegoats of the urban poor rioting in the name of Islam, and in other countries through the region. Foreigners are only indirectly at risk from riots, which are generally directed against local enemies.

MILITANT ISLAM

The example of the Iranian Shia Muslim revolution has inspired many other Asian Muslim activists, both Shia and Sunni. Iran has provided physical assistance to certain Muslim groups, notably the Moro National Liberation Front (MNLF) who have been fighting a secessionist guerrilla campaign in the southern Philippines since 1972, and factions in Indonesia and Malaysia.

In 1983 the Iranian Consul General in Karachi, Pakistan, was asked to leave after he had been filmed inciting local Shias to violence against the majority Sunnis. Libya also aids the MNLF and a Muslim secessionist group in Thailand, the Pattani United Liberation Organisation (PULO).

All orthodox Muslims agree that the government must rule according to the precepts of Islam but the impact of the Iranian Revolution will be blunted by the divisions within Islam. Pakistan is a case in point. The Shias, the community most susceptible to Iranian propaganda, are a minority of at most 20 per cent. Pakistan is the only country in the world created specifically for the sake of Islam yet President Zia ul-Haq's Islamization programme is opposed by the Shias, because they think it is too Sunni-oriented, and even by Sunni conservatives, either because they think Zia is exploiting Islam for selfish political ends or because they regard his reforms as insufficient. Meanwhile Pakistan's long-standing social and ethnic divisions remain unresolved. All participants in the Pakistani debate will try to recruit Islam to their cause – even the late Prime Minister Bhutto claimed to practise 'Islamic socialism' – and some will use violence but the specific role of Iranian subversion will remain peripheral.

By population Indonesia is the largest Muslim country in the world but the great majority are *abangan* Muslims, much influenced by ancient Javanese Hinduism, as opposed to *santri* orthodox Muslims who are themselves divided. A nationwide popular Islamic revolution on the Iranian model is therefore not feasible but Islam may also be used as a rallying cry by, for instance, the urban poor who feel that their interests are being neglected. Thus a minority of Muslims will continue to demand a more overtly Islamic government and an even smaller minority will advocate the use of force. Such factions are likely to target the Chinese community, perhaps by bombing their property, as well as the government.

Malaysia has produced violent, and transitory, Muslim terrorist fringe factions but the most important Muslim political force is the opposition Pan-Malaysian Islamic Party (PAS). PAS leaders, who are Sunnis, have visited Iran 'to learn the Iranians' fighting spirit, not their Shia faith'. Outright Islamic revolution is unlikely but Islam's new assertiveness could prove destructive in a society where the Muslim Malays hold only a narrow majority over the mostly non-Muslim Chinese and Indian communities.

Small violent fringe groups, often sponsored by Iran and Libya, will be active throughout the Islamic world, and beyond it, over the next ten years. The offices and embassies of recalcitrant governments will be first in the line of attack but less well-guarded commercial premises could also become symbolic targets. As a revolutionary force of wide popular appeal Islam is most effective where, as in Iran, it can combine religious appeal with nationalism and a demand for social justice. No group in south or east Asia is close to achieving such a combination.

MINORITY SECESSIONIST MOVEMENTS

Violence between rival ethnic groups in Asia is as old as Asian history. The compulsory peace of the colonial period suspended but did not resolve such conflicts and in many cases the colonial powers prepared the ground for future disputes by demarcating borders which had been blurred or non-existent, thus formally linking isolated peoples, such as the Nagas of North-East India, to metropolitan governments with which they had little or no previous association. In other cases the colonial authorities provoked new jealousies by favouring some groups at the expense of others or by encouraging the penetration of entrepreneurial minorities into new areas. Examples include the Indians in Burma and the Chinese in Malaysia.

While the theme is ancient there are several new factors involved in contemporary ethnic conflicts. First, governments are more centralized than before. Previously border communities were allowed considerable autonomy provided they acknowledged their allegiance to the central government and did not grant access to an enemy. Now with improved transport and communications, central governments have the means to play a more active role in their outlying areas. Strategic imperatives and the desire to develop forestry or mineral resources provide incentives to do so. But government intervention, even in the cause of development, frequently provokes a local backlash. Thus in Pakistan the Baluch, whose main function in the British period was to act as a buffer against

Afghanistan, have fought four insurgencies since 1947 against what they regard as Punjabi interference from Islamabad. Resentment persists in spite of and partly because of the government's new development schemes. Secessionist activity will continue well into the 1990s and could again erupt into insurgency.

A second new factor is the unprecedented force of demographic pressure which has forced large-scale migrations into previously undeveloped areas and, again, provoked backlashes from the local people. Large numbers of Bengalis from both Bangladesh and the Indian state of West Bengal have migrated to Assam and the neighbouring states, threatening to outnumber the indigenous peoples in their own homelands. In Assam the backlash has been particularly bloody: 4000 people, mostly Muslim Bengalis, were massacred in February 1983. In Bangladesh itself the Shanti Bahini is fighting a guerrilla campaign to prevent settlers from the plains overwhelming the homelands of Buddhist minority tribes in the Chittagong Hill Tracts. There is no easy solution either to the economic pressures which forced the Bengalis to migrate in the first place or to the fears of the Hill peoples; there is therefore every prospect of deepening agitation and further massacres, perpetrated by either side.

Whereas most of the Bangladeshi settlers are illegal, in Indonesia the government itself is sponsoring a huge transmigration scheme to settle three million Javanese on to the other islands of Kalimantan, Sulawesi and Irian Jaya (West Papua) over the next five years. The government's purpose is partly economic, to alleviate overcrowding on Java, and partly political, to hasten the integration of the highly disparate cultures of Indonesia. In Irian Jaya in particular the government has taken on a 'civilizing mission' to force the indigenous Melanesian population to adopt a more 'modern' way of life: some have responded by joining a small, poorly armed guerrilla group, the Free Papua Movement (OPM). They have no hope of success but conflict will continue in Irian Jaya and the late 1980s could see new movements in the other islands.

Partly in reaction to external pressures the minorities themselves are developing a greater sense of 'national consciousness'. By tradition the Baluch of Pakistan, the Nagas of North-East India and the Melanesians of Irian Jaya are each divided into several tribes. Now many, especially the younger and better educated, are acquiring a more unified Baluch, Naga or Melanesian 'national identity', and this will harden their resistance to outsiders.

There is also a trend towards the political radicalization of beleaguered minorities. Among the exceptions are the pro-Western, Baptist-led Karen National Union in Burma but the experience of the previously unpoliticized Tinggian tribe of the Philippines is more typical; they were readily recruited by the leftist New People's Army after peaceful protest had failed to stop a destructive logging project in their homeland. Another example comes from the Tamils of Sri Lanka. The moderate Tamil United Liberation Front is rapidly losing support at the expense of Marxist–Leninist Tamil guerrillas because its non-violent strategy has failed to achieve autonomy – or restrain undisciplined government troops. The alienation of the Ceylon Tamil community has brought about an insurgency, which, at best, will drag on for years in the north and, at worst, could lead to an island-wide conflagration.

Some separatist groups have achieved a degree of *de facto* autonomy while still living under the threat of government offensives. The various insurgent factions of Burma control about 40 per cent of the country's territory but they are inhibited by regular government campaigns. The Burmese government spends some 35 per cent of its budget on defence, but neither the government nor the separatists have any realistic prospect of ending the stalemate. Since the Second World War there has been only one successful internationally recognized, secessionist movement in Asia – Bangladesh, which had support from India. This will continue to be the pattern for the next decade. Separatists will go on fighting but only those who can attract external support have a significant chance of success.

It is just conceivable that India may invade Sri Lanka in support of the Tamils, with catastrophic consequences for Tamils in the south of the island, or that the Soviets may attempt to set up a puppet 'independent' Baluchistan. Both of these are still very much worst case scenarios. The chances are that today's map of Asia will still be valid in ten years' time.

THE COMMUNIST INSURGENCIES

During the 1970s India faced a short-lived and ineffective rebellion by the Naxalites, officially known as the Communist Party of India Marxist–Leninist, centred in Bihar and West Bengal. The Naxalites remain active in isolated pockets only and they have no prospect of instigating large-scale rebellion in the next ten years. South-East Asia will remain the principal arena for communist insurgency.

In the wake of the Second World War every South-East Asian country faced a communist revolutionary challenge, but only in Vietnam did the communists succeed in establishing themselves as the principal nationalist movement. Elsewhere they frequently were, and are, weakened by their association with national minorities. Initially the various parties benefitted from the external support of both China and the Soviet Union but the value of these links has been greatly reduced by the Sino-Soviet split, which brought corresponding splits in local parties, and its geopolitical consequences, especially China's quarrel with Vietnam and the Kampuchean conflict. China will continue to oppose the Vietnamese-sponsored Heng Samrin regime in Phnom Penh by sending arms to the infamous Khmer Rouge, the largest of the three Kampuchean resistance groups. Five years of dry-season campaigns have not brought either side close to victory; nor will the next five years. An end to the conflict must be found by diplomats rather than guerrillas. So far this prospect is remote.

The Kampuchean conflict has brought some benefit to Thailand: China has withdrawn support from the Communist Party of Thailand (CPT) partly because it needs the Thai government's acquiescence to continue supplying the Khmer Rouge. This has been one factor in the CPT's decline from 12 000 guerrillas in the late 1970s to some 2500 in 1985. Among other factors are splits within the CPT – younger members see the rigidly Maoist leadership as 'un-Thai' – and, most importantly, the government's highly successful counter-insurgency strategy which combines military pressure with offers of economic assistance to rehabilitate defectors. A few CPT rebels will remain in the jungles. Others may return there if rehabilitation schemes prove disappointing. The Thai government has identified a new threat from the Phak Mai group based in Laos but this is unlikely to develop significantly. Small bands of rebels, Muslim separatists and criminals as well as communists, will linger on in the jungles into the early 1990s but without presenting a serious challenge to the Bangkok government or to business.

Some 2500 guerrillas from the Communist Party of Malaya (CPM) and an antagonistic splinter group will resist joint Thai-Malaysian counter-insurgency campaigns in the two countries' border areas for years to come but the CPM has no hope of playing a significant role in Malaysian national politics. Its leadership has always been Chinese and many of its rank and file members are now Thai. Despite radio propaganda designed to appeal to a Muslim audience it remains a fringe movement with no hope of attracting substantial following from the majority Malay community.

The Burmese Communist Party has now turned to opium-running to compensate for the reduction, but not cessation, of Chinese logistical support. With 12 000 guerrillas it is the largest of the Burmese insurgent groups but has little prospect of ending the current military stalemate.

The only South-East Asian communist insurgency which is actually growing is the New People's Army (NPA) in the Philippines. It now has some 12 000 guerrillas and much larger support base in two-thirds of the country's provinces. With no significant external aid it is following a long-term strategy of political education, building up its rural support in order to take over the cities in the 1990s. The Marcos regime has entered its last phase and the divided liberal opposition is struggling to rebuild democratic institutions against the threat of a military take-over. If the military do take over, the NPA will benefit from further political polarization. Even under a civilian regime the parlous condition of the country's economy (GNP declined by 5.4 per cent in the first half of 1984) will continue to erode the political centre. NPA supporters already include disaffected churchmen and members of the middle classes. A Sandinist-style take-over by the 1990s is entirely plausible.

TARGETS, TACTICS AND PROSPECTS

The primary targets of both separatist and communist guerrillas will be the personnel and installations of the government against whom they are rebelling. Attacks on these targets will range from bombs against individual politicians, soldiers and government servants to full-scale insurgencies. Some groups, for instance the Sikhs campaigning for a separate state in the Indian Punjab, will sabotage infrastructure targets including railways and canals. Foreign companies may be included in the government category when they are working with the state on joint ventures.

Insurgent groups lacking external support use various methods to raise money. The Karen National Union levies a 5 per cent tax on black market goods passing from Thailand to central Burma. In the 'Golden Triangle' of northern Burma, Thailand and Laos, several groups, both separatist and leftist, exploit the narcotics trade. Elsewhere rebels make extortion demands on both local and foreign business. These range from 'revolutionary taxes', commonly levied by the New People's Army in the Philippines and the Communist Party of Malaya, to kidnapping for ransom, a favourite tactic of the Moro National Liberation Front.

Political kidnaps of foreigners are relatively infrequent but victims in 1983 and 1984 included a French couple taken by the Karen National Union in Burma, three Shell employees taken by the Shanti Bahini in Bangladesh, a Swiss missionary pilot held by the OPM in Indonesia and an American couple kidnapped by Tamils in Sri Lanka. For rebel groups such incidents have the merit of attracting world publicity. Plane hijacks are attractive for the same reason. In 1984 the Sikhs in India, with two successful hijacks and one attempt, were the most frequent perpetrators but other groups such as the Sri Lankan Tamils will be tempted to follow their example.

An assessment of political violence is, by its very nature, a one-sided analysis, selecting the factors which make for chaos rather than those which make for stability. Certainly large tracts of Asia will face continuing outbreaks of political and social turbulence. But not all. There is little to say about Japan because political violence there will be peripheral. Taiwan and South Korea face serious long-term external threats but, despite their authoritarian political systems, the fruits of economic prosperity should reduce the threat of violent dissent. China faces huge social problems and its stability is far from assured but its chances of finding it are better than they have been for most of this century. Given skill and statesmanship even countries like Sri Lanka and the Philippines will be able to reduce the threat of deepening political violence. No Asian country can afford to be complacent but nowhere are the problems insuperable.

Part III

Resource Papers

14 Terrorism in Western Europe

DR HANS JOSEF HORCHEM

THE PRESENT SITUATION

Terrorism was used successfully in such places as Algeria and Kenya to end colonial rule. But since then it has accomplished virtually nothing to achieve its long-range goals anywhere. In that sense, terrorism has failed. Yet terrorists persist. And that is the paradox that leads to increased bloodshed.

One should distinguish three kinds of present-day terrorism: terrorism motivated by ideology, left-wing or right-wing; terrorism of national, separatist or tribalist origin; and state-supported terrorism.

Terrorism which is rooted only in ideology without having support from outside does not have a chance of surviving. National or separatist terrorism has a chance to persist if it is not met by a combination of decisive law enforcement with possible political concessions. The problems for the future will be state-supported terrorism.

Both West Germany and Italy have dealt serious setbacks to terrorist organizations within their borders. Embassies and potential victims for kidnappings are better protected. Governments became more efficient in gathering intelligence and combating terrorism. Because of these successes by state authorities the terrorist organizations became smaller, making them tougher to monitor and penetrate. Terrorists turned to hit-and-run tactics rather than trying to seize and hold stationary targets such as an embassy or a parked airliner. An example is the Armenian ASALA, now perhaps the most active terrorist group. The Armenian extremists have assassinated 28 Turkish diplomats and their dependents and wounded 100 more in the last seven years.

There are many hypotheses that attribute contemporary terrorism to social, economic, political, and historical factors, but no single cause has been identified for the increase in the use of terrorist tactics throughout the world that began in the late 1960s. Generally, however, terrorist tactics have been adopted when other modes of armed conflict or peaceful means to attain certain goals have failed. By the late 1960s, it was clear that the rural guerrilla movements in Latin America inspired by the success of Fidel Castro and patterned on the Cuban model had failed. Leftist revolutionaries began to devote more attention to combat in the cities. Urban guerrilla warfare led almost automatically to the use of terrorist tactics. Great dramatic acts of violence in a major city win national, perhaps international, attention. It was an easy move from killing or kidnapping local officials to killing or kidnapping foreign diplomats.

Meanwhile, frustrated by the failure of the Arab armies in 1967 and unable to wage guerrilla warfare in Israel, the Palestinians launched a global campaign of terrorism against Israel and its supporters. When hijacking airliners provoked worldwide outrage, the Palestinians turned to seizing hostages at places like Munich and Khartoum. Terrorist tactics then were adopted by radical students in Europe, the United States, and Japan when the mass protest movements of the late 1960s failed to bring about the changes they sought.

In contrast to the increased constraints on governments in the conduct of war, terrorists have adopted the concept of total warfare – they recognize no civilian noncombatants. Terrorists may attack anything, anywhere, anytime. Over the past 15 years, the spectrum of terrorist targets has expanded to include diplomats, embassies, airliners, airline offices, tourist agencies, tourists, hotels, airports, trains, train stations, reactors, refineries, restaurants, pubs, churches, temples, synagogues, nuns, priests, the Pope, schools, students, and nurseries. This widening of the range of 'legitimate' targets and the resultant narrowing of the category of innocent bystanders parallels and extends the twentieth century concept of total war: In the

Second World War, all combatants attacked cities, factories, workers, anything connected with the enemy's 'war machine', and anything nearby.

THE GERMAN EXAMPLE: LEFT-WING TERRORISM

The arrest of the three RAF-cadre Brigitte Mohnhaupt, Adelheid Schulz and Christian Klar in November 1982 was significant as part of a process which started years ago. The decline of the RAF had already begun in October 1977 when the then leading group committed suicide in the prison of Stuttgart-Stammheim. After this the RAF could not meet the objectives for which it claimed to stand for. The reason for this were flaws in ideology and the wrong calculation in strategy. These failures in operations led to a loss of confidence among many of its sympathizers.

The failures of the RAF – after the culmination of its activities in 1977 – were already indicated by an unrealistic simplification of its strategic goals and by inadmissable shortcomings in its ideological views. In the beginning the RAF had primitively compared the situation in the countries of the Third World with the situation in the Federal Republic. The leaders of the RAF claimed also to speak and act for the working class, without having real connections with the working population. The support needed by a clandestine group of activists did not develop. The assaults of the RAF did not mobilize a revolutionary mass movement. The revolution was postponed into a far future. This Utopian principle could not mobilize new 'fighters'. After the arrest of Mahler and the death of Meinhof the RAF became more and more an organization which isolated itself and also its sympathizers into elitist arrogance. The later papers of the RAF, like the 'Heidelberg paper', seem to be nothing else than cries for help and solidarity.

The RAF could conceal the flaws between ideology and reality for a while by way of violent action. The death and the arrest of comrades-in-arms during the occupation of the German Embassy in Stockholm in April 1975 was the first important defeat of the RAF. After two years the RAF had recovered. The zenith of its criminal actions was in 1977. Members of the RAF murdered Attorney-General Siegfried

Buback and his bodyguards on 7 April, the banker Jurgen Ponto was murdered on 30 July, on 5 September they kidnapped Hans Martin Schleyer after killing his driver and bodyguards and then murdered him on 18 October.

But also this escalation of violence did not bring the mass-base the RAF hoped for. The RAF could not achieve its prime target to free the prisoners of Stuttgart-Stammheim. The government of the Federal Repbulic did not give in to this pressure. After a commando of the task force of the GSG-9 freed the passengers of the Lufthansa-airliner in Mogadishu, the leaders of the RAF committed suicide in the prison of Stuttgart-Stammheim. Since then the RAF has no longer had any convincing concept nor the success in operations which is the precondition for New Left solidarity in the field and for the recruitment of new comrades-in-arms. After that all operations planned and attempted by the RAF failed until 1985.

Three terrorists of the RAF who participated in the killing of Hanns Martin Schleyer rented a helicopter in 1978 to fly over the area between Heidelberg, Frankfurt and Wiesbaden. They prepared an attack against a facility of 'US imperialism', the US forces. When they realized that they were under surveillance they had to cancel their preparations and had to go underground again.

On 25 June in 1979 members of the RAF made an attempt to murder Alexander Haig, then head of the NATO forces in Europe, on his way from his home to the headquarters of NATO in Casteau near Brussels. The bomb which was aimed to kill him exploded only a split second after he crossed the bridge where the bomb was hidden.

On 31 August in 1981 a bomb exploded at the NATO air force base in Ramstein (Pfalz) and wounded 20 soldiers and civil servants. The attack was carried out by members of the RAF and aimed to destroy the headquarters.

On 15 September members of the RAF fired an anti-tank grenade and several gunshots into the car of General Frederick J. Kroesen, Commander-in-Chief of the US Army in Europe. The General and his wife received only minor cuts when the grenade, fired from a wooded hillside in an elaborately planned ambush, exploded on the boot of the car, partially shattering its rear window.

On 11 and 16 November 1982 the then leading terrorists of the

RAF (Brigitte Mohnhaupt, Adelheid Schulz and Christian Klar) were arrested. Weapon depots and caches for documents and money were discovered in Bavaria, Baden-Württemberg, Hesse, Lower Saxony and Hamburg. The RAF is now running out of arms, ammunition and money. The RAF will need a long time to recover from this blow, if it is able to survive at all. The decline of the RAF is also shown by the fact that several underground papers of other left-wing extremist groups are explaining the 'failures' of the RAF as the result of a wrong ideology and strategy.

Nothing succeeds like success. On the other hand, failures will produce more failures. During the period 1978–84 the RAF had tried several times to inflict another wave of violence on the country without success. Because of this it lost sympathizers. Besides that, German society is experiencing today another kind of decline, a social disease, which is threatening to demoralize society from within. A growing number of young people are becoming more and more unsteady and unstable in a complicated world of technology. They are alienated in a world of computers, machines and papers, and they are afraid of no longer having any influence over their own future. They are withdrawing from responsibilities and bailing out of society. They are not the recruits wanted by the RAF for terrorism.

In the political field the mood has changed, too. The impressive peace movement is also directed mainly against the United States but does not want to lose mass support by using violence. It is afraid of being discriminated against because of RAF action against US facilities and US military personnel. Terrorist actions during the time of 'peaceful demonstrations' in the autumn of 1983 were not attempted because they were regarded as being counter-productive for the RAF.

Finally, the RAF also finds itself rejected by the stronger and more numerous 'Revolutionary Cells' (RZ). The RZ are still a virulent terrorist power. Their policy was from the beginning to distinguish their strategy from the political concept of the RAF. They opposed the theory of the RAF that only student elites should guide the revolution. They emphasized that each action should be fed back to the 'masses'. Each single revolutionary activity should be tied to and brought into line with existing conflicts in society. Operating from these principles the RZ developed the so-called 'contact-theory'.

Until 1980 their attacks were directed only against objects. In 1981 the RZ admitted that human beings could also be hurt by the attacks. With the killing of Hans-Herbert Karry (Minister of Finance of Hesse) on 19 December 1980, the RZ gained a new profile. In a letter of confession the murderers claimed that the attack on Karry was only meant to be 'punishment'. They wanted to shoot him in the knees. They only killed him because it was too dark to aim correctly. The RZ obviously wanted to follow the Italian example with this type of attack.

After the killing of Hans-Herbert Karry the theoreticians of the RZ discussed exhaustively the problems of theory and practice. Anonymous articles of the RZ were published in some underground papers. The RZ explained that the death of Karry was an 'error'. A revolutionary group could mobilize 'masses' only when it could rely upon the level of the consciousness of the people; in the present political situation in Germany attacks against human beings would be counter-productive; therefore revolutionary activities of the RZ should for the time being be aimed only against 'objects'.

Regarding the political and economic situation in the last years the RZ concentrated its agitation on the 'Multinationals'. The multinational corporations became the incarnation of imperialism – following the propaganda of the RZ. Industrialization in the Third World, promoted by international capitalism, has brought the under-developed countries into even greater dependence on the industrialized countries than before. Today the countries of the Third World would rely almost entirely on the decisions for investment made by the 'Multinationals'. The profits of the multinational corporations would almost all be transferred into the capitals of the North and not re-invested into the Third World.

The classic models of Marxism explain imperialism as the result of contradictions inside capitalism. The theory of the RZ describes imperialism as a gigantic conspiracy of the 'Multinationals' against the peoples of the world. The chance to win new comrades-in-arms is diminished by this narrow-minded view of history. On the other hand the 'contact-theory' of the RZ and its determination to attack only objects and not human beings could motivate young people also to support the cause of the RZ in the near future.

Today 65 German terrorists are in jail; 29 of them are

members of the RAF; 20 belong to the former 'Movement of the 2nd of June' (unified with the RAF since June 1980), three are members of the RZ and 13 are right-wing terrorists. There are warrants for the arrest of another 29 wanted terrorists. 18 of them are members of the hard core of the RAF, eight belong to the RZ, two are stragglers of the 'Movement of the 2nd of June' and one is a member of the *Wehrsportgruppe Hoffmann*.

The 'legal environment' of the RAF is composed of about 150 members. Centres for their activity are Berlin, Hamburg, Frankfurt, Wiesbaden, Stuttgart, Heidelberg and a few cities in the Ruhr-area. RZ exist in Heidelberg, Frankfurt, Wiesbaden, Mainz, Bochum, Düsseldorf and Berlin. Altogether they have 150 members.

The fact that during the demonstrations of the peace movement in the Autumn of 1983 terrorist actions did not occur does not mean that Germany is not threatened by terrorism in the future. It is true that murderous attacks of the RAF will probably be regarded as counter-productive. The political climate in the Federal Republic has changed. The growing number of unemployed youngsters in principle is not a reservoir for future terrorists. New recruits for the RAF in the 1970s were mainly motivated by the ecstasy of the student movement, blossoming out of an affluent society. New economic restrictions and orientation to discipline within the student youth will lead to other results than to an escape into terrorist violence. On the other hand, the activities of the RZ will encounter a certain resonance in an atmosphere of anti-Americanism which is growing within German youth.

Finally all European countries have to cope with attacks from splinter-groups of the PLO and of the Armenian ASALA.

Terrorism of the RAF and of the RZ is anarchistic, no matter how its activists justify it subjectively. It challenges the State institutions responsible for security. They have to respond. Only a free democratic society acknowledges its conflicts, for its strength lies in this openness. The activists do not recognize that their actions are improving the standing of the security services, which for a long time were open to criticism. The resort to violence and anarchism is self-defeating. So long as the institutions of the State are supported by the vast majority of citizens this form of revolutionary conflict has no chance of success. This does not ensure that there will be no activists for the future. Mahler explicitly declared that the battle must be fought 'without a view to victory'. Ideologial conviction and a romantic feeling of solidarity with other fighters in other parts of the world will support the hard-core activists.

TERRORISM OF RIGHT-WING EXTREMISTS

In 1982 the security services of West Germany registered 64 violent actions by right-wing extremist groups. Twenty-nine of them were committed by neo-Nazi groups. In 1981 the security services registered 108 violent actions; in 1980 there were 113. This decrease of violent activities from the right is the result of the immediate response of the German security forces against any sign of rightist extremism. The police and the law courts, in particular, have reacted quickly, decisively and with energy.

Neo-Nazi terrorists' activities and their techniques of acquiring weapons and explosives using bank robbery to finance their crimes, maintaining safe houses and establishing links with foreign terrorists, are copied from left-wing terrorists. The Nazis have tried to adapt some terrorist methods pioneered by other groups to their own purposes. But the Nazi potential for violence and terror is inherent in their ideology and fanatical hatred.

The trend of increasing terrorist activity by the extreme right in Germany since 1980 caused deepening concern to the government. In May 1981 five members of the 'National Socialist Action Front' were arrested at Lübeck on charges of murdering a homosexual whom they thought to be a traitor. The following months Karl-Heinz Hoffmann, leader of the banned *Wehrsportgruppe Hoffmann*, was arrested and charged with establishing a criminal organization. His group, with an estimated 400 members in several states (Länder) of the Federal Republic, had long been under police surveillance and was suspected of involvement in the 1980 Oktoberfest bombing. Evidence also emerged that Hoffmann's group had been involved in terrorist links with splinter groups of the PLO, including sending neo-Nazis on training courses and trading in used vehicles. In August 1981 came the issue of warrants for the arrest of Hoffmann and his friend, Franziska Birkmann, on charges of murdering the Jewish publisher, Shlomo Levin, and his companion Frieda Poeshcke in Erlangen. Hoffmann is said to have given the order for the assassination. The killer was Uwe Behrendt, member of the *Wehrsportgruppe Hoffmann*, who committed suicide after going back into Hoffmann's training camp in the Lebanon.

Five members of another neo-Nazi terrorist group, the *Volkssozialistische Bewegung Deutschlands* (VSBD) or People's Socialist Movement of Germany, led by Friedhelm Busse, were involved in a shoot-out with police in Munich on 21 October 1981. Two of the neo-Nazis were killed, one injured and two arrested; two policemen were injured. The VSBD – in the meantime banned – was based in Munich and has attracted support from fanatical neo-Nazis both in Bavaria and across the rest of the country.

In December 1980 one of Busse's young followers, Frank Schubert, was involved in a gun-fight with Swiss customs officers who caught him trying to smuggle arms across the Rhine. Schubert killed two Swiss officials and then took his own life.

The VSBD has had around 600 supporters. In August 1981 it planned to set up a branch in Hanover; 40 neo-Nazis were arrested after fighting in the city centre of Hanover. Among those arrested were a Frenchman and six British soldiers. The VSBD and the other neo-Nazi terrorist groups in the Federal Republic do not have any significant following among the electorate. Nevertheless the very existence of such militant groups, with their capacity for terrorist attacks on the innocent and for spreading the poison of racialism 40 years after the defeat of Hitler, is deeply disturbing.

The main reason for the growing militancy and the increasing of violence within the small neo-Nazi organizations in the last few years is probably the decline of the NPD. The process of decay which experienced this 'old' party of right-wing extremists worked as an injection to some of the neo-Nazi groups. The prohibition of the *Wehrsportgruppe Hoffmann* and the VSBD brought stragglers of these organizations together. They founded the latest terrorist organization, the 'Kexel/Hepp-Group'.

On 18 February 1983 police arrested three neo-Nazis in the Frankfurt area and two neo-Nazis, belonging to the same group, in London. A resident of a flat near Frankfurt had given to the police the first hint that some 'strange things' were going on in a neighbouring flat. The police started surveillance for several days and later detected in the apartment, masks (probably to use during bank robberies) and chemicals to construct bombs.

When three members of the group came back to their safe house they were arrested: Dieter Sporleder (22), Hans-Peter Fraas (22) and Helge Karl-Wulf Blasche (40). Fraas was a member of the *Wehrsportgruppe Hoffmann* since 1977 and – before the organization was outlawed – working as *Unterführer* (sergeant). He was responsible for military training of members of the *Wehrsportgruppe Hoffmann* in PLO camps in the Lebanon and became the leader of a *Wehrsportgruppe Libanon*. Blasche was a member of the VSBD since 1980. Sporleder was the leader of this group in Hesse since 1978.

In London Walther Kexel (23) and Ulrich Tilman were arrested. They were both members of the outlawed *Wehresportgruppe Hoffmann*. A sixth member of the neo-Nazi group, the student Ottfried Hepp (25), escaped. One of the men arrested confessed. Because of the information given by him, the police discovered two weapon caches in a forest near Dietzenbach (Hesse) with four shot-guns, two pistols and revolvers.

The distance in ideology and targets between right-wingers and left-wing terrorists is obviously declining. The neo-Nazi Eduard Wolfgram, killed in October 1981 by police in Munich, said: 'The anarchists have the same aim as we. They will destroy this state, and exactly the same aim I have.' Pamphlets against 'Soviet and US imperialism' of right-wingers and left-wing terrorists are showing more and more similarity. The RAF and the RZ are combating 'US imperialism' and the 'Multinationals'. The members of the 'Kexel/Hepp-Group' were fighting for an 'anti-imperialistic Nationalism to liberate Germany'. They say 'that we have the same targets as the IRA, the ETA, the PLO and as Gaddafi'. They understand themselves as 'national revolutionaries' and 'National Socialists'. The models they want to follow are not Hitler and Göring but Gregor Strasser and Ernst Röhm, the leaders of the social-revolutionary wing of the National Socialists. Walther Kexel and Ottfried Hepp wrote in a common letter: 'We are neither right nor left. We want neither an American state nor another Soviet-Republic in Germany.'

Public opinion poll surveys show that about 13 per cent of the electorate of West Germany tend to be extremist, either to the far left or to the far right. This figure may be true for almost all democratic societies. For Germany this means around three million people are viewing history and politics very much through National-Socialist lenses. This large minority hates democracy, pluralism and all foreign minorities. It is also unshaken in the belief that violence is not only inevitable and necessary, but also that it is a cathartic and cleansing force. A more hopeful finding of these studies was that those below the age of 40 are largely immune to these extreme right-wing views; the highest concentration is, not surprisingly, among the over-50s who fought in the war. This does not mean, of course, that the activists and terrorists of the new extreme right are of that age. Most of them are between 20 and 30 and possibly only influenced by this climate of opinion.

One important break-through came in June 1982 when two neo-Nazis of the German Action Group were sentenced to life imprisonment by a Stuttgart court for carrying out seven bombings and arson attacks in 1980, including those in which two Vietnamese were killed and two Ethiopians injured. After the arrest the police discovered over 20 arms and ammunition caches in the Lüneburg Heath. They included anti-tank weapons, pistols, rifles, 30 000 rounds of ammunition, and a large store of hand grenades.

Despite this climate inside a minority of the German population the chances for right-wing terrorism in Germany are very limited. The main attraction of neo-Marxism–Leninism and Maoism for young people is that they offer scientific criticism, rewarding discussion and meaningful agitation; in their broad outlines, their dialectics and operational techniques are easy to learn. The extreme right has no such intellectually persuasive ideology. What it once had was destroyed by the demagogic Third Reich. Political theories and ideology based on racial supremacy are nonsense in an increasingly egalitarian world. That nations should have equal rights is a fundamental principle of the United Nations; decolonization progresses irresistibly and the new states increasingly determine the interests even of the Superpowers. No country, unless it has the intention of working against its own interests, can promulgate a policy of racial supremacy in today's world. Such a policy, whatever the individual's sensibilities or thoughts, would be doomed from the start. This is perhaps the main reason why one of the basic principles of right-wing extremism is no longer viable.

Any attempt to resurrect anti-semitism – the most extreme form of racial thought and German chauvinistic ideology – would be impossible, particularly given the trauma of the Nazi-era. There is a minority among the 'Old Right' which denies that past events ever happened, but on examination of their motives, it is normally seen that an admission of acceptance would threaten their very existence.

Thirty years after the collapse of National Socialism the effect of it and of Fascism in discrediting all right-wing extremist traditions is more apparent than in its immediate aftermath. In Europe, at least, this has made the successful re-establishment of a similarly totalitarian right-wing extremist system virtually impossible. Authoritarian régimes existed in Portugal and Greece, for example, but both collapsed in 1974. Spain became a democracy too, after the death of Franco. It would be foolish to suppose that there is no international contact between the various right-wing extremist groups, but in Europe there is no such movement with a governmental power base, with ideas for managing crises; nor is there any movement able to sustain or support in any practical way right-wing extremist movements in other countries.

The overwhelming majority of the German population regards the right-wingers more or less as 'incorrigible criminals'. The rather small neo-Nazi groups are lacking sufficient recruits and financial support by other political groups. The fact that they are now moving into bank robbery only confirms this estimation. Their attempts to establish international cooperation are mainly last ditch efforts aimed at survival. The use of more and more violence to the point of murder is in principle significant for the process of decline. Even if they are open to cooperate with left-wingers, for example with the 'Revolutionary Cells' (RZ). they will be rejected by them. But they are always in a position to be misused as mercenaries against 'US imperialism' and 'Zionism' by Palestinian organizations.

NATIONAL AND SEPARATIST TERRORISM

The situation of left- and right-wing terrorist organizations in Italy is more or less the same as in Germany. Both are in a general process of decline. More than 2000 members of the Red Brigades, the *Prima Linea* and *Ordine Nuovo* are in jail. This is probably the result of the increasing efficiency of the police forces and the result of the confessions of the *petenti*, members of terrorist organizations who are willing to confess, for instance, repenting of their deeds, therefore hoping to be free from punishment.

There are hints that Gaddafi is trying to support an 'independence-movement' on the island of Sardinia with money and weapons. If he succeeds this will not be a national or separatist terrorist movement but a state-supported one.

In France left-wing *Action Directe* is now without the support of the Palestinians. If the PLO, who are becoming independent from the Syrians, were to start to help or to participate again in actions of *Action Directe* this too could be called state-supported terrorism.

Terrorism in Brittany remained the cause of a rather small minority. The Corsicans are clinging traditionally more to violence and 'vendetta', than the other parts of the French population. Their terrorism will persist as long as the French centralized government does not meet it with concessions on the way to more autonomy. In Occitania unrest has just started. The repression of the desire to use the own language and to have an own school system, combined with growing unemployment in the region could also lead to violence.

ETA terrorism is losing the importance in the Spanish Basque provinces it had two years ago. Members of ETA have killed more than 350 people since 1968, half of them police officers and members of the *Guardia Civil*. Admission to more autonomy of the Basques by the Madrid government is working against terrorism. The Basque authorities, now starting to operate with a genuine Basque law-enforcement organization, claims to be able to destroy ETA within the next four years.

The real threat for the near future will continue to be state-controlled terrorism.

TERRORISM SUPPORTED BY GOVERNMENTS

The relationship between governments and terrorists is not a simple conflict between terrorists and their patron states on one side and governments opposed to terrorism on the other.

Governments have at various times, (sometimes simultaneously) tolerated, combated, fomented, supplied, and exploited terrorist groups. Beneath the rhetoric of moral outrage is a labyrinth of secret wars and secret deals, of direct action and deliberate inaction.

As modern conventional war has become increasingly impractical, terrorists offer a possible alternative to open armed conflict. Nations that are unwilling or unable to mount a conventional military challenge – for example, Libya or Syria against the United States – have seen terrorism as an alternative. What began as a tactic of desperate and weak political extremists, has increasingly become a component of armed conflict among nations – a mode of surrogate warfare.

The US government has officially identified four nations that aid terrorism: Libya, Syria, Iraq and South Yemen. On the basis of public statements by American officials, several more nations can be added to the list, including, obviously, the Soviet Union, Bulgaria, East Germany, Czechoslovakia, Iran, Cuba, and Vietnam. If we also include countries that provide training, North Korea, and Algeria join the list; and adding countries that provide financial support to organizations that frequently use terrorist tactics brings in Saudi Arabia, Kuwait, and to varying degrees the entire Arab bloc of nations.

To a degree this kind of terrorism has become institutionalized, part of the system. This is not to say that terrorism is accepted, but rather that it is simultaneously combated, tolerated, and exploited in the same fashion that piracy was combated, tolerated and exploited by the European powers in the seventeenth and eighteenth centuries. We will have to live with it, and we will have to fight it.

15 Policing a Britain Under Threat

SIR ROBERT MARK

CRIME AND PUBLIC ORDER

My first task is to say something about the reality of what is loosely called law and order, and in doing so I suspect I may shatter a few long cherished illusions. Most of you will have formed a general impression that effective law and order depends on an efficient and honest police force serving an effective justice system. The crime novel since Sherlock Holmes, the cinema and television screens, even the news media, will throughout most of your lives have promoted a general belief in both, encouraged by lawyers, journalists and even some policemen.

This is not true. There never has been any reliable evaluation of the effectiveness of the police in the justice system and only in recent years have the curious begun to suspect that whilst the police and the courts have an important part to play, their importance lessens in relation to some crimes which are now so commonplace that they are accepted as part of the pattern of our daily lives.

Thus, for example, in Britain crimes against property, burglary, theft and so on, have increased steadily whilst the proportion cleared up decreases. And this at a time when the police have more manpower than ever before and expenditure on police is increasing at about 20 per cent per annum. Burglary, once a serious crime triable only in the higher courts, is now so common that the chances of successful detection in London are now less than 10 per cent. Moreover, of those burglars caught 70 per cent are under 21 and the remainder are men of straw.

The trend is therefore for the public to improve their crime prevention measures and, in particular, to insure against loss; though we are now reaching a stage at which some insurance companies are considering refusal to insure loss from premises in certain areas. For the great majority of those suffering losses from theft and burglary the police and the courts, through no fault of their own, are virtually irrelevant.

A similar situation is to be found in relation to offences against public order, arising from political demonstrations, strikes, football and other hooliganism, and racial tensions. The most the police can do is to contain them, sometimes with great difficulty.

The courts are even less effective. Delays in trials, the uncertainty of controversial evidence, the vagaries of juries, the fact that defendants are seen as token representatives of many who are never prosecuted, all these factors discourage prosecution or encourage acquittal. The justice system depends for its effectiveness on a high degree of unanimity. That may be forthcoming in relation to crimes which offend public opinion, but not in cases involving politics or race. There is even a growing tendency to regard crime prompted by those reasons as not really criminal. The only possible conclusion is that it is not violence itself which determines the effectiveness of the police and the courts. It is the *cause* of the violence which does that. Thus a football hooligan will be arrested, convicted and sentenced with scant ceremony, whereas a violent picket or demonstrator, or a coloured youth involved in a riot is unlikely to be convicted, or at the worst, will be given a sentence derisory in relation to his offence.

The effectiveness of the police and the courts for dealing with crime is subject to the same general consideration, namely, the extent to which the public as a whole is genuinely hostile to crime, assuming of course, a police ability to exploit that by operational efficiency and good public relations. Even a literate, tolerant society like ours, finds some types of crime unacceptable, notably murder, rape, child molestation and in particular, terrorism, whether politically or commercially motivated. The police will be helped by a sympathetic public hostile to the wrong-doer, and the probability of conviction by the courts will be greatly enhanced. Unfortunately the success rate in dealing with this very small number of newsworthy crimes, 98 per cent in the case of homicide, reinforces the misleading impression of the general effectiveness of the police and the courts in relation to crime generally.

COUNTER-TERRORISM: POLITICAL AND TECHNICAL CONSIDERATIONS

It is against this background, rather than the complacency with which the police and courts are viewed by the uninformed or the prejudiced, that I will try to explain the remarkable success of counter-terrorism in Britain. I should first explain that the nature of our society itself is relevant to the probability of terrorism, and to success or failure in dealing with it.

By the nature of our society, I mean the social, economic and political conditions in which we all live. Where there is an unbridgeable gulf between government and governed, between rich and poor, where the police are generally detested and feared and the courts regarded as a tool of government, where franchise is not universal and the government self-perpetuating, there you are likely to find terrorism. And there, also, it is likely to flourish. Authoritarian police methods and ruthless governments may confine it, but they will not defeat it.

Where on the other hand, a liberal democracy is based on universal franchise, plurality of political parties, freedom of expression, generous social welfare, and a general acceptance, if no more, of the police and justice systems, terrorism is much less likely, and when it occurs, more easily defeated. In other words, I believe that the social conditions on the British mainland heavily favour the security forces in countering terrorism, because they are democratically accountable and enjoy almost universal support in discharging that particular task, a support which would be, of course, less certain if the task was more controversial. That is the essential condition for countering terrorism, without which the most efficiently organized, trained and led security forces could not succeed.

It may be thought that conditions in Britain might

understandably have led to a very low priority for anti-
terrorism, for the numerically small police force, unable to do
much about the ever-mounting crime wave. That this is not so, is
largely due to the IRA and to a far-sighted police appreciation of
the problems likely to arise from aircraft hijacking and hostage
taking for political reasons. As long ago as 1974 Scotland Yard
had taken the initiative by inviting opinions from experts on
kidnap, ransom, extortion and bombing from many countries,
including the United States, and if not then certain of the
measures it should take, proceeded to give high priority to
contingency planning.

It was well understood that the general freedom of Britain
from crime of that sort was no guarantee for the future. After
all, any government can now be subjected to the pressures of
kidnap, ransom and hijacking in support of causes entirely
outside its own jurisdiction. An embassy siege or aircraft hijack
in Britain may be followed by demands upon foreign
governments as distinct from our own. Indeed, the more civilized
and humane a country is, the more it is likely to be chosen as an
appropriate stage on which to influence world opinion. The
contingency planning which following this realization was of
great value. It established the basis for cooperation between
government, police and army, which allowed the first police–
army security exercise at Heathrow to pass without any
significant public hostility, and facilitated the close support of
the SAS in cases of extreme gravity. It also ensured the
acquisition of a variety of sophisticated technical resources, as,
for example:

- The creation of a central bank of information on kidnapping,
  extortion and similar crimes
- The provision of emergency communications systems, both
  line and radio, divorced entirely from conventional networks
  and with mobile out-stations
- Helicopter back-up
- Extensive improvement in technical support such as opto-
  electronic equipment for night work, photographic
  surveillance equipment, electronic detection and radio
  tracking equipment, listening devices and so on.

These facilities are not only available to all British police forces
but were freely lent to the *Garda Siuchana* during the siege at
Monasterevin.

THE ORGANIZATION FOR COUNTERING TERRORISM

Servicemen and police officers, however, will know only too well that the best possible equipment and the most intelligent contingency planning cannot in themselves guarantee success. The one factor essential to that, is a clear and universally understood pattern of administrative and political responsibility and an equally clear and unquestioned chain of command. That has not always been forthcoming and, indeed, against the historical and constitutional background of law enforcement in Britain, might be thought impossible. After all, government, police and army may be involved, lacking as they did recently, any experience of what might be called 'combined operations'. It is perhaps one of terrorism's most valuable, if unintended contributions to the stability of British government that this essential requirement has now been fulfilled. It almost certainly would not have been possible to achieve in less threatening circumstances.

The practical position is now as follows: England and Wales are policed by only 47 police forces, varying in size from 1000 upwards to the Metropolitan with 26 000 or more. There is, of course, a large technical and administrative civilian back-up. Conditions of service are identical in each force and interchange is essential to reach the highest ranks. Since 1964 the authority of a police officer extends throughout the whole country. Training and advanced training are undertaken commonly, and each force is able in emergencies, to demand mutual aid from the remainder. Each force, except the Metropolitan, is *administratively* accountable to a local police committee, appointed by its constituent local authorities and magistracy, but is free from interference in law enforcement. The Metropolitan police force is administratively accountable to the Home Secretary, but enjoys the same operational freedom as other forces. There are, however, important safeguards in that the power of the police to prosecute is subject to, in a small proportion of cases, the consent of the Director of Public Prosecutions (DPP) or the Attorney General, and it is in the power of the latter to assume the responsibility for any prosecution if he considers that necessary to the public interest. The Attorney General is, of course, a member of the government. It is thus possible to ensure that in exceptional cases of national rather than local importance, the views of government which would ordinarily have no influence at all in the prosecution process, can be given full weight, or, indeed, can persuade or force a decision, in the making of which in the general run of cases it would not even be consulted. This is particularly relevant to terrorist incidents involving the national interest.

The operational resources and powers of the police are therefore common throughout the whole country, as are the constitutional safeguards provided by the powers of the DPP and the Attorney General. No matter where a terrorist incident occurs, the reaction of the police will reflect a common national policy. The involvement of the army in support of the police conforms to the same pattern. Anyone of the 47 chief police officers can appeal to the Home Secretary for military aid. If the Home Secretary approves, he will seek the consent of the Minister of Defence. Troops already highly trained for this kind of work are then made available under their own command system but in close cooperation with the police. In the most serious cases, the Cabinet Office Briefing Room (COBRA) will be set up, thus enabling immediate decisions to be made in the light of police, army and political representation.

The system works extremely well because it obviates doubts and uncertainties, avoids disagreements about jurisdiction and ensures that the national interest is not excluded from decision-making. The activation of COBRA is not essential. It depends on the circumstances and potential threat of each incident and, of course, on whether the government is directly or indirectly involved through the actions or demands of the terrorists. Its very existence has nevertheless eliminated the uncertainty hitherto affecting the reaction of the security forces to this kind of crime. It is one area of government planning which, admirable in concept and efficient in practice, does not attract the attention of politicians and journalists ordinarily suspicious or critical of any measures falling under the heading of security, because it is successful.

THE POLICE AND THE MEDIA

Operationally, therefore, a chief officer of police faced with a terrorist situation is unlikely to be caught unawares. His relations with other forces, the army, or the government are predetermined. The weaknesses of the laws and the judicial system, and, in particular, the reaction of the public are unlikely to afford him any insuperable problems. Probably his most anxious responsibility is to gain the confidence and cooperation of the Press.

This can be very important. The extent to which a well equipped and well led police force can defeat extortion by kidnap or bombing may be determined by its relationship with the news media. Public interest in such crimes is intense and the media respond accordingly. This can mean that the police – and perhaps the families and employers of kidnap victims – are faced with the problem of how to ensure the goodwill and cooperation of the media, or at least dissuade its representatives from behaviour which might endanger the life of the victim or prevent an arrest.

Whatever the legal or moral entitlement of the police to the cooperation of the victim in the investigation of ordinary crimes, they have to accept that in protracted crimes in which the life of the victim is at risk, victims, employers and the public itself are entitled to demand that information they impart to the media shall not be revealed without regard to their interests and that the activities of investigative reporters shall not increase the risk to the victims or impede the attempts of the police to effect their release and arrest the wrong-doers. This requires a reasonable certainty that the means of communication between police and press are secure and that editorial–managerial agreement with the police is not undermined by unauthorized leakage.

The resultant dilemma is seemingly insurmountable. The basic function of the Press in a free society is disclosure, whatever the consequences. Moreover, it is not an entity. It is a highly fragmented, competitive institution whose members, if denied information unreasonably, will vigorously seek to obtain it by unorthodox methods, themselves arousing hostility and resentment. In pursuit of their legitimate aims, as they see them, journalists may behave in a way that contributes to the suffering of the victim or even to his death, aggravates the suffering of his family and the anxieties of his employers, and frustrates the efforts of the police.

It is therefore of incalculable importance and encouragement that since 1975 the Press has shown the same aversion to kidnapping and extortion as the public generally and a consequent willingness to regulate its own activities in the interests of saving life. Since then it has on three or four occasions complied with police requests to withhold information about kidnaps. Each case ended with the safe recovery of the victim and the prosecution of the wrong-doer. This unique self-denial in so competitive an industry on an issue of such potential news value is an indication of the detestation with which the Press itself regards kidnapping. It is one of the strongest reasons for believing that happily for us, in this country it is a crime without a future.

Let it be cleary understood, however, that those favourable conditions for the security forces did not create themselves. They result from contingency planning, preparedness, training, experience, and cooperation. Police, army, government and, on rare occasions, the Press, may all have a part to play, and mutual trust, a clear pattern of command and accountability and a supportive public are the principal factors in ensuring its present success.

16 Political Violence and the Response

ASSISTANT COMMISSIONER JOHN DELLOW

THE SPECTRUM OF POLITICAL VIOLENCE

As the Metropolitan Police was in part born out of political violence and since 1829 has found itself continually having to deal with it at varying levels, I find some difficulty in fixing a starting point for this Chapter. If for no other reason than that of lack of space, I will choose 1970. That year and since has the added advantage of being relatively fresh in our memories and provides an interesting range of subject matter to review. However, it is fair to point out that no matter at which point in police history one addresses this subject the definition spectrum of police interest and responsibility is wide – wider than that of almost any other agency – and is likely to look very similar no matter at which point in time one chooses to look at the subject.

Graded in terms of obviousness but not necessarily in terms of impact, volume or importance the definition and responsibility spectrum of political violence with both small and large 'P', looks something like this:

- Exploitation of an existing instability in the community (eg, bad housing, unemployment, crime. A specific issue that divides a community).
- Initiating instability for Political Purposes
- Political Demonstration accompanied by Violence planned or unplanned
  (that is likely or unlikely to arise). This may develop from or be part of the first two points.

- Violent Acts against property short of lethality
These include super-glue in locks of fur shop by animal rights activists. Stone-throwing etc, at buildings, paint-daubing and other offensive attacks. This is sometimes related to racial attacks and sometimes accompanied by the risk of personal injury.
- Violence to the person short of lethality
Besides forms of assault and wounding this will include kidnapping accompanied by threats of further violence and even death.
- Violence to property by means of lethal weapons
For example bombing of buildings accompanied with warnings or at times or places where personal injury or death is unlikely but inevitably a risk.
- Violence by lethal means directed at persons and/or property
Such as bombings, assassinations, hostage taking, hijacking or violence against property and person without care as to whether or not injury or death results. This can include anything from a violent attack by terrorists with arms to take hostages to low capacity letter bombs or incendiary devices sent to persons inspired to support political objectives in the narrowest sense.

From this you will see that the police service is required to use very wide definitions of both 'political' and 'violence' if it is to fulfil its responsibility properly.

DEMONSTRATIONS AND RIOTS IN LONDON SINCE 1970

Let us now look at the years since 1970 in the light of that spectrum. Of the first two parts, exploitation of and the initiation of, instability within the community the first is I think a reality and the second may or may not be so but certainly it is possible and therefore requires noting.

Exploitation of instability is probably a well-tried tactic in many fields of subversion but I will refer only to how it seems to be manifesting itself in London in recent years. We identify what appear to be calculated moves at times to undermine systems and authority and achieve political changes – small and large 'P' – by means outside the accepted democratic system. Typically this can happen in areas of poor housing, high unemployment, high crime rate and in areas where there is a high fear of crime brought about by visible signs of disorder, such as vandalism, graffiti and decay; untypically it might happen elsewhere. Such moves may result in violence either between sections of the community or towards the police when they attempt to maintain or restore order.

In some parts of London where certain offences ranging through illegal drinking and drug trafficking to violent street crime are common, police intervention is sometimes met by crowd gathering and violence towards the police to intimidate them and maintain the social condition desired by some of the local community. Inappropriate action by police under such circumstances can lead to conditions of extreme disorder and even riot. If police do not wish to trigger disorder out of all proportion with the original offences and yet still discharge their responsibility to enforce the law then the action of arrest and/or the bringing of offenders before a court, police intervention has sometimes to be delayed. Thus, we see acts of violence having an effect on policing methods (if not ultimate objectives). Under such circumstances the opportunity for exploitation for more sinister or more directly political purposes is considerable and obvious. Under such circumstances even the ultimate objectives of police could be at risk.

We have also seen during the last decade efforts by groups, sometimes supported by individual politicians, to cast doubt on the correctness or appropriateness of accepted institutions or agencies for discharging specific civic responsibilities. An example of this is the coroner's inquest. Several times in the last few years we have seen the suitability of the inquest challenged as a means of establishing the cause of death or a desire to go beyond the objectives of the inquest. On occasions this has resulted in demonstration, sometimes having political support by individual politicians and sometimes political involvement by the non-parliamentary political parties. Violence has not always been excluded at such demonstrations.

Let me turn now to major political demonstrations which are accompanied by violence or the risk of violence. During the decade or so to which I refer we saw the growth and eventually to a degree, the decline of the conflict on the streets between political extremes. We saw in the mid-1970s the extreme right march through Lewisham, its confrontation by the extreme left and the consequent violence to each other and to the police by both. This occurred in other places in London, such as Southall and in other parts of the country. We saw something of it associated with the 1979 elections. The same elements manifested themselves at industrial disputes and what might have been relatively ordinary flexing of industrial muscle sometimes degenerated into public disorder and violence on a mammoth scale.

The desire for political demonstration by the extreme right continued in the 1970s and was almost always met by opposition by the extreme left and *vice versa*. The right wished to march in Central London and in places of some sensitivity. For example, Lewisham was again chosen during a by-election, Peckham in South London was another and on one occasion in the East End of London the roles were somewhat reversed when several thousand Asians wished to demonstrate against the extreme right and march past the offices of the National Front.

The police strategy became one of allowing both sides to demonstrate but separately. The judge's words about escape routes and converging marches in the Red Lion Square Inquiry were burned into the souls of police Commanders. We learned that to preserve the basic but unwritten right to demonstrate and yet preserve order by separation was a delicate exercise and extremely expensive in manpower and other resources. You will remember the phalanxes of police officers used to contain and protect marchers and the strong cordons of foot and mounted officers used to seal off assembly and dispersal areas and the route between. More manpower was needed to sweep the routes of opposition and contain it at places where it could demonstrate but without risk of confrontation and consequent violence. This did not always prevent violence towards police. In general, however, the tactics proved successful and demonstrations did take place in the most sensitive areas without disorder but at the cost of deploying thousands of police officers per demonstration and the temporary curtailment of liberty for many law abiding local residents and business people.

This seemed to work. As the sensation of violence receded and to many extremist demonstrators the point of demonstration lost, so the number of such events declined.

After the Brixton disorders in 1981 there was a resurgence of the desire on the part of the extreme right to march and demonstrate in sensitive parts of London such as Brixton and places where similar but lesser outbursts of disorder had occurred. The disorders had produced another dimension to policing generally and political demonstration in particular. The tactics of allowing demonstration but kept in check by large numbers of police now clearly contained the risk of sparking off serious disorder within the community of the area of demonstration as well as from counter-demonstrators. Under such circumstances there would be no readily identifiable and containable opposition. Therefore, recourse to banning marches under the 1937 Public Order Act was made. Although policing a ban on marches is sometimes more difficult than policing the intended march, on the whole this has worked.

Now, however, we see the growth again of civil disobedience – last seen in the 1960s – which sometimes becomes violent – by intent or not who knows – for political ends and police are having to reassess strategy and tactics in this field.

BOMBING, ASSASSINATION AND HOSTAGE-TAKING

Now I want to deal with the more spectacular end of the spectrum. Bombing, assassinations and hostage-taking. Mention has already been made of the tendency in the past few years for factions of otherwise quite unmilitant and politically unaffiliated causes to use letter bombs and incendiary devices and this may be a continuing and disturbing pattern. Similar tactics, of course, continue to be used to further the causes of known and declared terrorist organizations. Thus, we find some very strange bedfellows in this field of political violence or terrorism.

We saw a very intense campaign of bombing in London in the early and mid-1970s perpetrated by a diversity of terrorist organizations and this was coupled with assassinations. In consequence the Metropolitan Police responded by an operation in Central London designed:
- to prevent terrorist activity, and
- should it be unsuccessful in this regard, apprehend terrorists if attacks took place.

This resulted in the Balcombe Street siege.

You will remember that terrorists carried out an attack on a building in Central London with firearms; were seen by police; chased to Balcombe Street where they occupied a flat and held hostages. At that stage, it was the most serious operation of its kind that the Metropolitan Police had experienced and valuable lessons were learned. It allowed for Government liaison to be tested, although compared with later events the degree of sophistication of political and governmental issues involved was slight. It also tested contingency plans which resulted in subsequent refinement.

Terrorist bombings and political assassinations continued through the late 1970s but much more sporadically and although there remained a diversity of organizations responsible one began to see a shift of emphasis away from the Irish dimension to what one might refer to as 'other', that is, Middle Eastern, Armenian and even domestic. This has continued up to the present day where the balance in terms of volume is certainly in favour of non-Irish based activities.

In 1979 and 1980 as well as the domestic political street violence to which I have already referred, we experienced several incidents of note and which may have had a significant effect on terrorism in the capital. There were two particular political assassinations both of Middle Eastern origins, one at the Mosque in Regents Park and one at a mews in Kensington. In each case as a result of excellent street police work by police constables the murderers were caught within minutes of the crimes. In the first instance, because of rise in tension and threat assessment, good planning had resulted in enhanced uniform foot patrolling in the vicinity of the Mosque. Upon the assassination taking place within the grounds of the Mosque two young unarmed police officers patrolling nearby heard the shots, saw the assassin, gave chase and arrested him within a few minutes and two hundred yards of the crime.

The other incident concerned a police officer driving a police vehicle in Knightsbridge. He heard the description of a suspect connected with the murder in a nearby mews being passed over the police radio network. Within 30 minutes of the murder the police officer identified the suspect, by the description, waiting at a bus stop in Knightsbridge. He called for assistance and again unarmed police arrested the suspect who subsequently proved to be the murderer.

THE SEIZURE OF THE IRANIAN EMBASSY IN
LONDON IN 1980

Thirdly, in 1980 the occupation and taking of hostages took place at the Iranian Embassy in Princes' Gate. This was in many ways different from what we had ever experienced in London, or I believe, elsewhere in the mainland of this country. Of the more important differences were:

- The number of terrorists and hostages was greater than experienced in other sieges – criminal or terrorist.
- It was a planned operation by the terrorists whereas other similar events were spontaneous acts during the course of escape from criminal activity.
- The size and character of the building involved was quite different from previous buildings. It presented a much harder and tougher target.
- The international politics presented considerably more complexity for negotiation.
- There was a strong element of martyrdom both on the part of hostages and the terrorists.
- The terrorists were intellectually superior and likely better prepared and well equipped compared with those criminals dealt with at previous sieges.
- The scale and intensity of the police operation was greater than anything we had experienced up to that time.

This is not to say that there were no similarities with previous experiences or indeed with exercises conducted to test planning. There were and those allowed the contingency to work well but the differences tested our flexibility and impressed upon us that as the Iranian Embassy siege differed from previous experience so will future incidents differ from the Iranian Embassy operation. Thus emphasizing the need for good contingency planning accompanied by a strong element of flexibility.

In the event the operation became unique in that the military was not only deployed in support of the police but was committed as part of the operation. Much of the success of the operation from beginning to end, including the total governmental support of the police with no political intervention at operational level, and the military action was due to a close personal knowledge by the Police Commander, the Government Liaison Officer and the Military Commander of each other gained during joint planning and exercising prior to the event. This allowed a very close and effective working arrangement with quick decision-making at the scene.

From this operation we learned a great deal about many aspects of siege management. We learned much about logistics; the resource requirement to sustain the operation over the six days was considerable. We learned even more about negotiation, the art and the mechanics, especially in the context of international politics and, of course, we learned a little more about the news media and its potential effect on such operations. I would like to refer to this aspect in more general terms shortly. I said that I thought these three incidents – the assassinations and the siege – were significant. After the Iranian Embassy siege I thought one of two things was likely to happen. Either that the success of both police and military and the resolution of the Government would act as a challenge or they would be a deterrent. It was possible that other terrorist groups would say 'we could take on the SAS and win'; 'those at Princes' Gate were ill prepared' or 'they were not resolute enough' or even 'we welcome martyrdom and London is the place to go'. This did not happen. Whilst one must never be complacent about such things it would seem that the alternative occurred. The deterrence of the Princes' Gate operation was enhanced I think by the rapid arrests in the two assassinations to which I referred and which occurred relatively close in time to the siege. These events together with other successes and with the avowed governmental policy of 'no capitulation' to terrorists, underlined the message that went out that London – and by association other places in this country – was a hard target for that kind of operation. It is unlikely I think that it had much effect on the other forms of terrorist activities. Memories become dim, however, and May 1980 is now history so we must remain vigilant and prepared.

THE MEDIA AND TERRORISM

I do not wish to dwell on the Princes' Gate operation too long. However, I would like to make a reference to the news media and communication generally.

Of all police operations concerned with criminal activities, Princes' Gate was better covered by television and sound broadcasting than any. In fact two members of BBC television were hostages, a BBC reporter was used alongside a negotiator in contact with the terrorists; BBC World Service was actually used to publish a statement by the terrorists as part of a hostage release package and considerable facility was granted by police to all news media both national and international in order that it might do its job. In addition we experienced infiltration by at least one newspaper which was thwarted and, of course, the now world famous television pictures taken of the military preparations immediately prior to its assault on the Embassy – the implications of which were and are obvious to all.

Since the operation all these aspects of the news media activity and their implications for future operations have been considered by police and I am sure the Army. I conclude that this is an issue that will always pose problems for the police and army commanders. However, in addition I have let my mind wander to future possibilities which I think are equally important. I am no technologist but I have been examining the potential of satellite and cable television.

I have two issues in mind. Firstly the lack of local control that a police commander might have at the time of an operation in respect of satellite television transmission. No matter what sort of accommodation he has with his local television operators the ability in the future to transmit and receive domestic television internationally as a matter of course, introduces a very high level of risk to the operation which will present the commander with little room to manouevre. The second relates to the ability of tomorrow's terrorists' groups and their supporters to become television programme makers and feed their product via satellite and cable to many different locations. At present the public's main concern seems to be with the matter of taste; will cable and satellite television present us with a stream of idiot quiz shows and computer produced soap operas? will the system be exploited by pornographers? and so on. If we can be concerned quite properly about this aspect of television it seems to me that those of us interested in the subject matter under discussion might give a passing thought to the possibility of exploitation for purposes of propaganda and preparation in the field of political violence and terrorism. I put this no higher than a point for debate and examination, if it is thought that a link exists.

CONCLUSIONS

In summary then what has the last ten years or so taught us? Firstly, it has reinforced a known fact which is that the police interest and responsibility covers a very wide spectrum and our definition of 'political', 'violence' and 'terrorism' has to capture many anti-social activities which at first sight might not readily be categorized as political violence let alone terrorism.

We find that the extreme politics in street violence by way of organized demonstration has declined somewhat. That social conditions have in any event caused police sometimes to change tactics in this area. Recent civil disobedience is beginning now to re-emerge representing an old problem with some additions. Some of the energies previously expended in street demonstrations might have been transferred to the exploitation of causes.

We have seen a gradual change of balance in the volume of terrorist activity between that which could be said to be Irish oriented and that of other groups. Now we see the balance very much weighted on the side of the non-Irish groups. This is an interesting fact when considering the application of the Prevention of Terrorism Act that has been operating over the last few years.

In connection with such activities as assassinations and hostage-taking, successful and resolute action by Government, Army and Police, and a degree of success by the Police alone, might have spelled out that the UK is a hard target and might have acted as a deterrent to others. The Metropolitan Police has most certainly learnt that contingency planning, exercising jointly with other agencies and flexibility are very likely the corner-stones of success when it comes to real operation.

Lastly, the fact that, although the beginning of the 1980s has been considerably quieter than the beginning of the 1970s in terms of bombing, it still happens and can well go on doing so and in this respect we can never relax.

17 Maintaining the Democratic Process and Public Support

PROFESSOR PAUL WILKINSON

TERRORISM AND DEMOCRACY

The nature of terrorism is that it is both use of violence against the innocent and a psychological and political weapon which, usually in concert with other tactics, is used to overthrow the democratic system and to control the population. Most terrorist groups realize that public support for democratic values and institutions is a major obstacle to their schemes. Hence the democratic process is a key target. It is impossible to win the battle against terrorism by purely security or military measures. Nor are political and socio-economic methods by themselves enough. The trick is to harmonize strategy on both the security and political fronts: this is the only basis for a winning strategy.

In countering terrorism, however, the democratic state confronts an inescapable dilemma. It has to deal effectively with the terrorist threat to citizens and the state itself without destroying basic civil rights, the democratic process, and the rule of law. On the one hand the democratic government and its agencies of law enforcement must avoid the heavy-handed over-reaction which many terrorist groups deliberately seek to provoke: such a response would only help to alienate the public from the government and could ultimately destroy democracy more swiftly and completely than any small terrorist group ever could. On the other hand if government, judiciary and police prove incapable of upholding the law and protecting life and property its whole credibility and authority will be undermined. This is what happened in the tragic case of Lebanon from the mid-1970s onwards. The sovereignty and authority of government became meaningless as the country became a patchwork of warring fiefdoms. Thus in dealing with any serious terrorist campaign the democratic government must walk the tightrope between under- and over-reaction, with the added complication that the tightrope is pitched at different heights and angles in each case.

Another major problem of democratic response is that the security forces must operate at mid-levels of coerciveness, firmly within judicial, humanitarian and constitutional constraints, while their terrorist opponents, who do not hide their contempt for such restraints, can wage their struggle with utter ruthlessness. But despite these inherent problems of the democratic response there are no grounds for despairing of democracy ever defeating terrorism. It is a fatal illusion, assiduously fostered by terrorist propaganda, to assume that the gun and the bomb are bound to succeed unless the state suspends democracy to suppress terrorism. Such defeatism has no firm historical basis. Moreover it clearly plays into the terrorists' hands.

WEST GERMANY AND ITALY

The myth of the invincibility of terrorist movements should have been finally shattered by two recent success stories of democracies defeating terrorists: West Germany and the Baader–Meinhof and Italy and the Red Brigade. In both cases the democratic process, public support and the rule of law all withstood both the terrorist assault and the strains and stresses of response. Democracy survived, not without bruises and pains, but intact in all essentials.

How was this done? In both countries successive governments retained overwhelming public support for the main policy aims regarding terrorism; the preservation of democracy and the rule of law, the defeat of the terrorists' campaign and bringing terrorists to justice. The model they gradually learned to apply in both cases was the firm and consistent application of judicial control. Both governments were aided considerably by the full support and cooperation of all major political parties and institutions in the battle to defeat terrorism. (In Italy even the Communist Party remained true and determined in this cross-party cooperation).

Of equal importance were the practical measures taken to strengthen the police and intelligence services in countering terrorism. Coordination and command and control of anti-terrorist operations were considerably improved. West Germany made great strides in the computerization of data on terrorism. In both countries a new breed of 'supercop' emerged, with specialist knowledge and skills to lead the anti-terrorist battle, and standards of police training and performance were improved at all levels. Specialist elite squads were established to deal with particular tasks, such as hostage rescue. Italy and West Germany also introduced a limited range of emergency powers to strengthen the police, for example increased powers of search and detaining for questioning. In Italy there is no doubt the special decree permitting plea-bargaining by 'repentant' terrorists greatly increased the flow of intelligence which helped the police track down the Red Brigade cells. Last, but by no means least, one should bear in mind the effects of internal squabbles, ideological divisions and demoralization on the terrorist movements themselves.

Of course, it would be foolish to assume that the problem of terrorism has been totally eradicated in these countries. For example, West Germany still has the violence of the Revolutionary Cells, which have attacked US bases and industrial premises recently, the neo-Nazis who have bombed immigrants and other targets, and there are other extremists involved in terrorism. In Italy many neo-fascist terrorists are still at large. In addition there is the continuing problem that some Red Brigade activists have maintained their political organization within the gaols, and there is always a real danger that they will take up the struggle against liberal democracy when they eventually get out of gaol, even if under some other banner.

NORTHERN IRELAND

Despite these caveats no knowledgeable observer would deny that West Germany and Italy have achieved enormous successes against fanatical extreme left-wing terrorists. And in the light of these cases, many are bound to ask the question: Why can we not achieve similar success against terrorism in Northern Ireland? Why is it that in Ulster, despite the devotion and courage of the security forces, and their real successes in reducing the terrorist murder rate and in getting terrorists convicted and gaoled, the UK government seems to be losing the key battle for public support and the democratic process?

There are, we must recognize, special factors beyond any government's power to influence, which have helped to make Northern Ireland the worst protracted and bloodiest terrorist conflict in Western Europe since 1945. First, there is the intractable character of the 'double minority' conflict. The IRA is a self-styled 'national liberation' movement waging terrorism to 'liberate' a majority in Northern Ireland which adamantly refuses to be liberated. The militant Loyalist groupings within the Protestant majority in the North, for their part, remain hostile and suspicious of even the most tentative steps to power-sharing between the Protestants and Catholics in the North, for fear that this would be a stepping stone to unification with the Republic, in which they fear they would become a beleaguered and oppressed Protestant minority.

Second, we must not underestimate the problems created for the security forces by the long, winding, easily traversed border. It appears to be physically and politically impracticable to seal the border. The IRA can also rely on the support of some of its most militant traditional supporters in the border area. As the border can be so easily crossed by terrorists, the IRA can use sanctuary, logistic support, training areas and bases in the Republic to sustain a terrorist campaign almost indefinitely.

These facts alone make the Northern Ireland terrorist problem an exceptionally tough challenge for the British government and security forces, though one must concede that the cooperation with the Republic in patrolling the border area has strengthened considerably since 1978. Dr Garrett Fitzgerald's government is showing more determination than any other recent Dublin administration in attempting to suppress IRA and INLA terrorism south of the border.

But it must also be said that the United Kingdom's failure to defeat IRA terrorism after 14 years of bitter struggle is at least partly due to errors and omissions by successive British governments. Unfortunately the present government is no exception.

NEED FOR A CLEAR POLITICAL AIM

A fatal flaw is the government's lack of a clear political aim, other than the defeat of terrorism. In the eyes of the public, both in Northern Ireland and the mainland, the political leadership appears uncertain and divided over the political status and future of the Province. Therefore government finds it difficult, if not impossible to mobilize public support. There is no clear sense of direction or leadership on the Northern Ireland issue. Northern Ireland is not given a sufficiently high priority by the Prime Minister and Cabinet. This may seem inexplicable considering the huge costs of the conflict in lives and treasure and the fact that terrorism frequently spills over on to the mainland. It appears that Her Majesty's Government as a whole does not realize the reality or the gravity of a threat of all-out civil war in Ulster. (Mr James Prior once warned of 'a Cuba' in Northern Ireland. A more apposite example would be Lebanon in the 1975–76 Civil War).

The only recent Prime Minister who gave Ulster the priority it deserved, at least for a time, was Mr Edward Heath. And his government came closest to a lasting solution of the political problems of the Province, in the shape of the Sunningdale Agreement and the power-sharing Northern Ireland Executive with the Official Unionists and SDLP working together in government.

The irony is that Mrs Thatcher has got a comfortable parliamentary majority and a clear term ahead of her. Her party is not dependent on Ulster Unionist votes in the Commons. Mrs Thatcher has the reputation for enormous determination and energy in dealing with major political crises, as illustrated in the Falklands conflict. Unfortunately for Northern Ireland her interest in their plight seems sympathetic but extremely spasmodic. When she returns to Westminster from her brief forays to the Province the problem seems to get pushed to the 'back-burner'. Unless she decides to put her own personal style of leadership into tackling the problem, no major success will be achieved. It must also be sadly admitted that Mr James Prior, despite his sincere and devoted efforts during his tenure as Secretary of State, did not enjoy the clear confidence of the public and community leaders in the Province. This was a fatal weakness.

Most serious of all, the Government is totally failing to harmonize its security with its political strategy. The Provisional IRA, on the other hand, has been cleverly using its propaganda wing, Provisional Sinn Fein, in a dual-track strategy 'the ballot box in one hand and the Armalite in the other'. By using murder and massacre-with-elections the PIRA leadership stands to gain what it could never gain by murder alone – a victory for terrorism. This becomes sadly a more and more real danger as the SDLP (the non-violent party of the Catholic minority) becomes demoralized and fails to achieve anything at the purely political level. The effect of Provisional Sinn Fein winning a clear majority of the Catholic vote in Northern Ireland would be to totally polarize the politics of the Province. It would completely destroy the middle-ground and the capacity for compromise, which characterized relations for example, between the Official Unionists and the SDLP in the days of the Northern Ireland Executive.

It is an outrage, in my view, that a terrorist movement that openly boasts of its murders and of its determination to go on bombing and gunning its bloody way into power, should be allowed to use the democratic privilege of contesting elections for public office. Have we forgotten that these were the tactics used by 'legality' Adolf Hitler in the 1930s when he concerted the electoral tactics of the NSDAP with the street terror of the storm troopers? It is time we stopped this scandal of the Provisional murderers, through their Provisional Sinn Fein cover, masquerading as legitimate politicians.

I would not propose proscription as such: it would be in any case impracticable to prevent them publishing their propaganda or holding meetings of supporters. But what I would strongly urge is that the law governing elections be changed *so that any party that refuses to publicly disavow the use of violence would be prohibited from contesting elections for public office.*

It is urgently necessary for the Prime Minister to place the

Northern Ireland crisis at the top of her own Agenda and, with the aid of the Cabinet, to decide swiftly on a clear long-term political strategy.

I was one of those who strongly supported Mr James Prior in his efforts to establish the Northern Ireland Assembly. The basic idea of producing a vehicle for achieving partial devolution and ultimately a degree of power-sharing was brave and admirable. But we must now face the fact that this effort has failed. It was crippled from the outset by the SDLP's refusal to take its seats. Then the Assembly was rendered totally irrelevant by the petulant withdrawal of the Official Unionist Assemblymen. What is the point of providing a forum for the bickering sectarian parties of Northern Ireland if they do not have sufficient sense of responsibility or regard for the welfare of the whole nation, to at least participate in the deliberation of a parliamentary assembly?

Now that this worthy effort has failed the Government should declare its clear commitment to the only other practicable political arrangement. For as long as the Ulster majority wish to be joined with the United Kingdom political integration and continuing direct rule from Westminster is the only option that makes sense. It has the following advantages:

- It gives an unambiguous reassurance to Ulster's Protestant majority that their political status is not going to be sacrificed or bargained away. This will enhance public cooperation and support for Government Security Forces.
- It sends a clear message to the IRA and INLA murderers that they have *lost* the long-term political battle and this will serve to demoralize them even more than the 'supergrass' system has already. It thus tangibly helps the security forces.
- It ensures that the rights of *both communities* in Northern Ireland are properly protected under Westminster and Whitehall, in a manifestly *non-sectarian* system of administration.
- It does not preclude attempts to resuscitate and develop proper institutions of local government in the Province. (Incidentally this would put Ulster on exactly the same footing as Wales and Scotland – it is Stormont which was the constitutional anomaly.)

As regards the overall direction of the struggle to defeat terrorism in Ulster, I believe a tough new 'General Templer' style overlord is required to pursue a fully integrated political and security strategy and to coordinate the adminstrative and security machine at all levels. This post should replace the present post of Secretary of State until the emergency is ended and order is restored. This overlord director of the anti-terrorist campaign should have the total support of Prime Minister and Cabinet and direct access to Number 10 Downing Street.

The Ulster administration and security forces should be specially exempted from the public expenditure cuts and limits imposed on other Government departments. I firmly believe that a totally new policy of the kind described is needed – and needed urgently – if terrorism is to be defeated in Northern Ireland. A clear and practical policy of this kind would have the effect of restoring confidence among the vast majority of the public on the mainland and a clear majority in Northern Ireland. There is no time to waste. The latest wave of murders has brought Ulster closer than ever to the brink of full-scale civil war. Is anybody in Whitehall listening, or are they all too busy fighting each other?

18 International Cooperation, Intelligence and Technology

MAJOR GENERAL PETER DE LA BILLIERE

INTRODUCTION

For simplicity I intend to take the British environment, political backcloth and legal structure on which to base this chapter and I intend to take a glance at three facets of anti-terrorist operations: international cooperation, intelligence and technology. Four basic components necessary in combating terrorism have been defined by Colonel James B. Motley. Prevention through diplomacy: deterrence through security: reaction through incident response and perhaps most important and most open for improvement, as I hope I shall show shortly, prediction through intelligence.

In England, Scotland and Wales and, perhaps, Northern Ireland, we have developed the most effective blend of political, military and police coordination and tactical cooperation in the world. This is our good fortune and it is certainly an example that many other nations strive to emulate. However, it is not a practical suggestion to transplant the British solution to other nations. Geographic and demographic differences make this difficult, if not in most cases impossible, and so do constitutional constraints such as the *comme possetatis*, which precludes the use of American troops for operations on American soil except by special Presidential decree. Political decentralization such as exists in federated states like Canada and Australia and, by no means least, the complications imposed on those countries who have adopted third or in some cases fourth forces, all ensure that our solution is not and never will be their solution. Of course there are practical aspects of the British solution that are eminently adaptable for use by our allies: our selection and training of counter-terrorist forces is the envy of many; and our tactics and equipment are studied and emulated by our friends – and no doubt when access is possible by our foes – around the world. Likewise we benefit from similar exchanges of information and experience developed by our allies and friends – and of course by our foes.

INTERNATIONAL COOPERATION

Since the early 1970s, which for the terrorists were heady days of success, we have witnessed a surge of international cooperation in the fight against terrorism. Few military or police seminars on the subject do not include allied observers and commentators. There is now a wide range of academic discussions where problems of containing terrorism are discussed at an international level. International political coordination and response to the terrorist threat is determined and effective, and (more surprising in this world of divided interest) formal political organizations and forums do exist to coordinate the fight against terror. Perhaps I should mention a couple of those in which the British are particularly involved.

First, there is TREVI (Terrorism, Radicalism and International Violence): this was a network set up during Mr Harold Wilson's period as British Prime Minister and it is a European Community based organization operating outside the Treaty of Rome. Originally it was established at a political level but it quickly expanded to encourage practical cooperation between security agencies and ministries to improve and coordinate the fight against terrorism. There is an annual convention at political level but the emphasis is on practical cooperation, and meetings take place throughout the year at various working levels with police, intelligence officers and others attending. Perhaps an example of the successful outcome of these conferences may be seen in the Le Havre incident when French authorities recovered and detained a sizeable shipment of arms destined for the IRA to use in Northern Ireland.

In a more global context there is less formal coordination. However the 'Economic Summit' (Canada, France, Germany, Italy, Japan, UK and USA) provides an unlikely forum for Western nations to disuss the threat posed by terrorism and by hijacking in particular. The Bonn declaration of July 1978 offered a set of guide-lines to governments on standards of international behaviour when handling terrorist incidents. One of the most important directions stemming from this declaration is the obligation on nations to deny the movement of terrorists from the country in which they have committed their crime. The United Kingdom has demonstrated its political determination in this respect when Prime Minister Thatcher stated that one of the principles of negotiation at the very start of the Princes' Gate siege should be that the terrorists were never to be allowed to leave British soil until they had atoned for their crime: and again when the Home Secretary, Mr Whitelaw, refused the East African hijackers at Stansted the option of repatriation before their arraignment under United Kingdom law.

I believe that the West now holds the political initiative in the war against terrorism and I am impressed and encouraged by the extraordinary international political harmony manifest in the fight against this world-wide scourge. However, I read with great interest a perceptive article in *The Police Journal* by J. R. Thackrah. He made two particular comments which are at some variance with my own views. He considered political harmony to be less than perhaps I have observed it to be – perhaps a whiff of the peculiar problems of Northern Ireland is to be seen as the cause of his reservations – and he further pointed out that judicial collaboration is less well developed than it should be. I would agree with him on the latter point.

INTELLIGENCE

You will not be surprised that I find less contentment with the intelligence situation and it is possibly in this field that there is the most room for improvement and the least chance of satisfaction.

On 6 May 1980 the Home Secretary gave authority to the request of the Commissioner of Metropolitan Police for the SAS to rescue the hostages in the Iranian Embassy at Princes' Gate. I suppose most people, and I include myself amongst them, would agree that in broad terms and certainly in military terms, the outcome of this grave decision by Mr Whitelaw was a success. But we must question whether it should ever have been necessary for him to take it. You could with justification argue that the very need to resort to the use of the SAS identified an intelligence failure. Why had the terrorists gained entry into the United Kingdom without discovery? Why did we not possess knowledge of the threat that they posed to the Iranian Embassy? Once they were in the Embassy why was it so difficult to gain detailed tactical information to ensure that the result would be a no risk operation – and so on? Of course I am presenting a simplistic series of rhetorical questions. These are normally the privileged preserve of the press, historians and those who have responsibility for commenting on events but no responsibility in their evolution. Intelligence has the power to prevent an incident taking place, but even if it fails at that stage it is vital to the success of the operation which follows. Since both terrorist and counter-terrorist forces are vying for it and denying it to each other it is certain that we shall never be satisfied that it meets our demands. If it were to do so then that would be the end of terrorism.

Broadly speaking we require intelligence at various levels. First, at a political and therefore international level. This must depend on the willingness of nations to pass information to each other and to possess the means to do so while it is timely and relevant. There is some cooperation in this field, but, even where there is the will to part with information (by no means always the case), there will still be some practical impediments. The extent of information required and available on terrorists, their movements, their equipment, their plans, their objectives, their supply and logistic arrangements, are of infinite magnitude. Computers may have eased the problem of storage and access to this vast stockpile of routine information but there remains the difficulty of identifying the vital clues from this stockpile and, of course, doing so with the timeliness necessary to take effective counteraction. When it all works we hear nothing of it as a terrorist is thwarted but when it fails then we are faced with an incident, and the need for yet more intelligence, that is, the second phase – tactical intelligence such as was required in early May 1980.

To take a judgement to authorize a police or military assault, a politician must assess the risks and the chances of success. The police or military commander must possess the most detailed information on such matters as terrorist strengths, weapons, location, and psychological state, to mention just a few of the subjects on which questions will have to be answered. Routine observation, of course, plays a vital part, day and night, and the press have hinted at the use of modern technology capable of seeing and hearing through walls and curtains – but there is a requirement for more and yet more technological aids to obtaining tactical intelligence. Lasers, light intensification devices, low-light television, listening devices and many other pieces of electronic equipment are but a few of the means in which we are not far beyond the first generation.

Having identified strategic and tactical intelligence as areas requiring undiminished, indeed, increasing efforts to improve upon let me conclude this section by emphasizing the need for the improvement of international trust and enhancement of common objectives in such a manner that the vital international cooperation in intelligence matters is forthcoming. Following on from this the need to improve bilateral cooperation between police forces, intelligence services and agencies and special anti-terrorist units will always remain an important factor.

TECHNOLOGY

I attended a recent lecture on defence technology and the speaker made the interesting observation that the span between 1980 and the 21st century equated to the span from 1914 and full technical re-equipment of our forces in 1936. As a cavalry man he felt sure that the debate conducted by his predecessors in 1914 was more concerned with the latest developments in nosebags rather than the evolution of the tank. With microchip technology in its infancy, I anticipate equally immense changes in military equipment over the next 20 years and there will be an increased need for foresight and conceptual thought if we are to develop this potential ahead of our enemies, let alone our friends. This is a prerequisite if we are to contain the battle against terrorism.

I believe there are fields of technology in which terrorist operations may be expected to develop: Information Technology, Weapons Technology and Equipment Technology.

Information Technology. Information Technology is of prime importance in the field of intelligence and I have already mentioned the increasing problems of access and extraction which will arise from the ability to store vast quantities of information. There will be an increasing demand for access to this pool of knowledge and high speed extraction will be of increasing importance. For example, it is already possible for a policeman on the beat to verify the ownership and other details of any car in the country within two or three minutes of his making a radio request. Similar requirements will develop in checking weapon numbers, the names and background experience of individuals possessing a record. Plans of buildings identified as being a threat will be required for transmission over Ceefax and other visual communication transmission systems. Photographs of identified terrorists will be delivered electronically to police and security forces at the scene of an incident and to immigration officers and customs when requested. Already the ability to see throughout the darkness period has advanced to the point of turning the blackest night into dusk and has revolutionized the role of the observer. We must expect electronic inspection of baggage and freight to offer greatly improved surveillance capabilities at airports, ports and other places of inspection.

Although these developments will and do work in favour of the authorities there is one area in particular where they may at best be said to be neutral. During the Princes' Gate siege a television reporter had managed to smuggle himself into the flats overlooking the rear of the building. It had been decided that the assault should commence on this aspect just because it was free from public and press gaze and there would be no chance of the terrorists watching the SAS abseil down the building to their entry points on television. This particular reporter possessed the latest in electronic cameras and was capable of transmitting events as they took place straight into the national television network. The television authority concerned claimed they had built in a delay to ensure these pictures did not result in a loss of security. However, a less patriotic editor might be expected to take a very different approach and place commercial interests first. In any case it is not the task of the editor to assess the tactical implications involved in the handling of the information he obtains. This instant transmission of events presents a new range of problems for those responsible for handling terrorist incidents. It is my belief that the press – or rather the UK press – can be expected to cooperate in incidents such as this, if the editors are treated in a responsible manner and taken into the confidence of the authorities so far as security permits. As an aside I believe the press, far from being competitors for information on terrorist incidents, can in fact be helpful allies – the British press that is. However, even if the authorities do not use the media the terrorists certainly will and we can expect the developments in information technology to assist them in this objective.

Weapons Technology. Let us now take a glance at the effects of technology on the weapons front. In my judgement it will be the security forces who have most to gain in this field. We can look for greatly improved night sights, for greater precision and penetrating effect from small arms – so essential in an incident where the terrorists may be in immediate proximity to innocent civilian hostages. However, small arms development is unlikely to offer dramatic improvements and it is in the field of disabling agents, be they gaseous or explosive in nature, that technology is most likely to develop in the terrorist and counter-terrorist field. Remote control of explosives by wire and radio are obvious areas for progress but this is as likely and indeed probably more likely to assist the terrorist rather than the authorities.

An area which I do not wish to become involved in but which cannot escape mention is that of nuclear, biological and chemical weapons. We must be thankful that terrorist organizations have failed to develop this area of weaponry but we cannot assume that they will continue to ignore it in the future and indeed there have been incidents already, though they have lacked success. Prevention, detection and neutralization must be the areas where the authorities develop their attention and great progress has already been made and can be expected to continue in this field.

Equipment Technology. The prospects for progress here are limitless and cover such things as improved individual protection, more varied assault equipment of lighter weight and greater capability – ladders, non-stretching ropes, improved breaching techniques are to name but a few. Medical advances are not to be ignored, particularly in saving life in incidents remote from hospital treatment and in the psychological field when negotiating with terrorists and in hostage management both in captivity and after release.

CONCLUSIONS

In conclusion let me pull together the three areas of politics, intelligence and technology. Governments round the world have recovered from the initial shock of terrorism as manifest in incidents such as that of the Munich Olympic Games. This operation in 1972 became the watershed of success for terrorists and it is this moment in the history of modern terrorism that may be said to have galvanized governments into policies of cooperation and of determined resistance to acts of political terrorism. This incident caused the Heath government of the United Kingdom to authorize the establishment of the Special Air Service counter-terrorist force. TREVI, the 'Economic Summit' and the Bonn Declaration have brought to bear a united front amongst civilized nations in the fight against terrorism. The practical effect of this cooperation is a reduction in the scope of terrorist incidents and it has denied the terrorist communities aspirations of political gain and blackmail on a grand scale.

Bilateral cooperation between police forces, intelligence services and specialist counter-terrorist units is harmonious and widespread but it is in the field of intelligence in all its aspects, collation, collection and dissemination that the greatest room exists for further enhancement and cooperation. The areas which offer the most scope for development by terrorists lie in the NBC field – we should remember that the threat of radiation or toxic release could be as effective in terms of blackmail as the actual event if we are not prepared with the technology and the public relations plan and the public education necessary to counter it. Other areas where little experience exists within the United Kingdom includes the diversionary and debilitating terror of pre-hostility operations and, of course, the suicidal incident.

The authorities hold the lead in the battle for technological supremacy but it is a battle that will never finish in this age of the microchip, the remote device, the dormant bomb capable of being activated after many months of lying buried, perhaps dug in several inches or even several feet underground. Our development in the technological field must be on several fronts: counter-equipment and detection devices to locate concealed weapons and explosives; the development of terrorist hunting gear such as low-light and no-light viewing devices; listening devices; and more accurate, silent and effective weapons.

The terrorist has lost the initiative but not the will to fight and unless we maintain our guard and continue to dedicate resources and manpower to fight him he may well regain it through the astute application of technology. Let us also remember that terrorism is not the art of the crank and the crook but frequently becomes the surrogate extension of politics as practised by governments who see decreasing profit in conventional warfare. I suggest that it is in this field that we can expect to see the greatest future development of terrorism.

Bibliography

Alderson, John, *Policing Freedom* (Plymouth: Macdonald and Evans, 1979).

Alexander, Y. and Kilmarx, R. A., *Political Terrorism and Business* (New York: Praeger, 1979).

Becker, Jillian, *Hitler's Children* (London: Granada, 1978).

Beckwith, Charlie and Knox, Donald, *Delta Force* (New York: Harcourt, Brace, Jovanovich, 1983).

Belson, William, *The Public and the Police* (London: Harper and Row, 1975).

Cline, R. S. and Alexander, Y., *Terrorism: The Soviet Connection* (New York: Crane Russak, 1984).

Clutterbuck, Richard, *Guerrillas and Terrorists* (Chicago and London: Ohio University Press, 1980).

Clutterbuck, Richard, *Industrial Conflict and Democracy: The Last Chance* (London: Macmillan, 1984).

Clutterbuck, Richard, *Kidnap and Ransom: The Response* (London: Faber and Faber, 1978).

Clutterbuck, Richard, *The Media and Political Violence* (London: Macmillan, 1983).

Cole, Richard B., *Executive Security* (New York: John Wiley, 1980).

Cordes, Bonnie, *et al.*, *Trends in International Terrorism 1982 and 1983* (Santa Monica: Rand Corporation, 1984).

Cox, Barry, *Civil Liberties in Britain* (Harmondsworth: Penguin, 1975).

Cramer, Chris and Harris, Sim, *Hostage* (London: John Clare, 1982).

Creliston, R. D. and Szabo, D., *Hostage-Taking* (Lexington: D. C. Heath, 1979).

Denning, Lord, *The Discipline of Law* (London: Butterworths, 1979).

Denning, Lord, *The Due Process of Law* (London: Butterworths, 1980).

Dobson, C. and Payne, R., *The Weapons of Terror* (London: Macmillan, 1979).

Dobson, C. and Payne, R., *The West Fights Back* (London: Macmillan, 1982).

Draper, Hilary, *Private Police* (Harmondsworth: Penguin, 1978).

Eichelman, B. *et al.*, *Terrorism* (Washington, DC: American Psychiatric Association, 1983).

Evans, Alona and Murphy, John, *Legal Aspects of International Terrorism* (Lexington: D. C. Heath, 1978).

Geraghty, Tony, *Who Dares Wins: The Story of the SAS 1950–1980* (London: Arms and Armour Press, 1980).

Goren, Roberta, *The Soviet Union and Terrorism* (London: Allen and Unwin, 1984).

Hamilton, Peter, *Espionage, Terrorism and Subversion in an Industrial Society* (London: Peter Heims, 1979).

Henze, Paul, *The Plot to Kill the Pope* (London: Croom Helm, 1984).

Herz, Martin F. (Ed.), *Diplomats and Terrorists: What Works, What Doesn't* (Washington, DC: Georgetown University, 1982).

Hewitt, Patricia, *The Abuse of Power: Civil Liberties in the United Kingdom* (Oxford: Martin Robertson, 1982).

Hoffman, Bruce, *Recent Trends in Palestinian Terrorism* (Santa Monica: Rand Corporation, 1984).

Hoffman, Bruce, *Right-Wing Terrorism in Europe* (Santa Monica: Rand Corporation, 1982).

Hoffman, Bruce, *The Siege Mentality in Beirut* (Santa Monica: Rand Corporation, 1984).

Jackson, Geoffrey, *Peoples' Prison* (London: Faber and Faber, 1973) and *Surviving the Long Night* (New York: Vanguard, 1974).

Janke, Peter, *Guerrilla and Terrorist Organizations: A World Directory and Bibliography* (Brighton: Harvester Press, 1983).

Jenkins, Brian M., Books and Pamphlets published by the Rand Corporation, Santa Monica, California:
A Strategy for Combating Terrorism (1981).
Combating Terrorism becomes a War (1984)
Combating Terrorism: Some Policy Implications (1981).
Diplomats on the Front Line (1982).
Hostage Survival: Some Preliminary Observations (1976).
Intelligence Constraints and Domestic Terrorism: Executive Summary (1983).
New Modes of Conflict (1983).
Should Corporations be Prevented from Paying Ransoms? (1974).
Subnational Conflict in the Mediterranean Region (1983).
Talking to Terrorists (1982).
Terrorism and Beyond (1983).
The Lessons of Beirut: Testimony before the Long Commission (1984).
The Psychological Implications of Media-covered Terrorism (1981).
Will Terrorism Go Nuclear? (1975).

Jenkins, Brian M. (Ed.), *Terrorism and Personal Protection* (Boston: Butterworths, 1985).

Kellen, Konrad, *On Terrorists and Terrorism* (Santa Monica: Rand Corporation, 1982).

Knowles, Graham, *Bomb Security Guide* (Boston and London: Butterworths, 1976).

Koch, P. and Hermann, K., *Assault at Mogadishu* (London: Corgi, 1977).

Laqueur, Walter, *Terrorism* (London: Weidenfeld and Nicholson, 1977).

Livingstone, Neil, *The War against Terrorism* (Lexington: D. C. Heath, 1982).

Lodge, Juliet (Ed.), *Terrorism: A Challenge to the State* (Oxford: Martin Robertson, 1981).

Mackenzie, G. *et. al.*, *The Security Handbook* (Capetown: Flesch, 1983).

Mark, Robert, *In the Office of Constable* (London: Collins, 1978).

Mark, Robert, *Policing a Perplexed Society* (London: Allen and Unwin, 1977).

Mickolus, Edward, *Transnational Terrorism: A Chronology of Events, 1968–1979* (London: Aldwych, 1980).

Miller, Abraham, *Terrorism and Hostage Negotiations* (Boulder, Colorado: Westview, 1980).

Moore, Kenneth, *Airport, Aircraft and Airline Security* (Los Angeles: Security World, 1976).

Moorehead, Caroline, *Hostages to Fortune* (New York: Atheneum, 1980), also published as *Fortune's Hostages* (London: Hamish Hamilton, 1979).

National Advisory Committee on Criminal Justice Standards and Goals, *Report of the Task Force on Disorders and Terrorism* (Washington, DC: US Department of Justice, 1976).

National Advisory Committee on Criminal Justice Standards and Goals, *Report of the Task Force on Private Security* (Washington, DC: US Department of Justice, 1976).

Parker, Donn B., *Crime by Computer* (New York: Scribners, 1976).

Pope, D. W. and Weiner, N. L., *Modern Policing* (London: Croom Helm, 1981).

Purnell, Susanna and Wainstein, Eleanor, *The Problems of US Businesses Operating Abroad in Terrorist Environments* (Santa Monica: Rand Corporation, 1981).

Royal United Services Institute, *Ten Years of Terrorism* (London: RUSI and New York: Crane Russak, 1979).

Tomlinson, John, *Left; Right: The March of Political Extremism in Britain* (London: John Calder, 1981).

Wardlaw, Grant, *Political Terrorism* (Cambridge: Cambridge University Press, 1982).

Whitaker, Ben, *The Police in Society* (London: Eyre Methuen, 1979).

Wilkinson, Paul (Ed.), *British Perspectives on Terrorism* (London: Allen and Unwin, 1981).

Wilkinson, Paul, *Terrorism and the Liberal State* (London: Macmillan, 1977).

Wolf, John B., *Fear of Fear* (New York and London: Plenum Press, 1981).

Yallop, H. J., *Explosive Investigation* (Harrogate: The Forensic Science Society and Edinburgh Scottish Academic Press, 1980).

Yallop, H. J., *Protection against Terrorism* (London: Barry Rose, 1980).

Index

Notes:
1. Unless shown otherwise, a country entry is deemed to cover also nationals of that country—France includes French.
2. Political movements are normally shown by the initials of their titles with the country in parenthesis—ANC (South Africa), though may be shown in full where this is considered to be clearer to the reader—Red Army Faction (RAF) and Red Brigades (BR). English translations are shown in the table of Abbreviations (p. xiii).

197